99

SUPER FUN, ?

Head-Scratching,

BRAIN-BOOSTING

BIBLE Trivia QUESTIONS for Kids

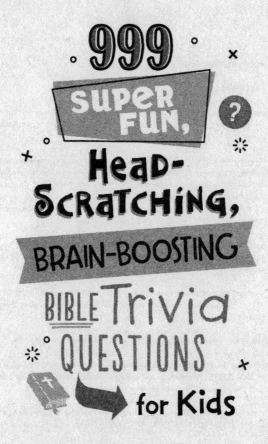

999 SUPER FUN, Head-Scratching, BRAIN-BOOSTING BIBLE Trivia QUESTIONS for Kids

Jodi and Lilly Simmons
with JoAnne Simmons

BARBOUR BOOKS
An Imprint of Barbour Publishing, Inc.

CONTENTS

INTRODUCTION

◇◇◇◇◇◇◇◇◇◇◇◇◇◇◇◇◇◇◇◇◇◇◇◇◇◇◇

Hi everybody! We're Jodi and Lilly Simmons. We're
sisters; we're ten and eight years old, and we LOVE to
LEARN about God through His inspired Word—plus
His people, His plans, and His purposes!

That's why we wanted to help put together a big
collection of trivia questions from the Bible. Some
of these questions might challenge and baffle you.
Some will be easy-peasy, maybe with some silly
thrown in! All of them will draw you closer to the one
true God as you learn more from the most fascinating
and powerful book on the planet!

Jodi and Lilly

BIBLE BITS AND BASICS

1. **FUNTASTIC FACT!** The Bible is the *bestselling* book in the world!

2. **Fill in the blank:** There are ____ total books of the Bible.

3. **True or False:** There are sixteen books in the Old Testament.

4. **True or False:** There are twenty-seven books in the New Testament.

5. **Can you name the books of the Old Testament?**

6. **Can you name the books of the New Testament?**

7. **What does the word *testament* mean?**

8. **FUNTASTIC FACT!** The Bible was written by over forty different authors: shepherds, farmers, tentmakers, physicians, fishermen, priests, philosophers, and kings. They were all under the inspiration of the Holy Spirit.

9. **What author wrote most of the Old Testament?**
   a) Adam
   b) Moses
   c) Noah while he floated on the ark
   d) Daniel while he was in the lions' den

10. What author wrote most of the New Testament?
    a) John the Baptist
    b) Mary
    c) Matthew
    d) Paul

11. FUNTASTIC FACT! The Bible was written over a period of some 1,500 years, from around 1450 BC (the time of Moses) to about AD 100 (following the death and resurrection of Jesus Christ).

12. What languages was the Bible written in?
    a) French and Spanish
    b) Pig Latin and Oompa Loompa
    c) Hebrew, Aramaic, and Greek
    d) Italian and Chinese

13. Who first translated the Bible into English?
    a) John Wycliffe
    b) Saint Nicholas
    c) Mother Teresa
    d) Martin Luther

14. When was the Bible first printed?
    a) yesterday
    b) 1800
    c) 1454
    d) 1492

15. What is the longest book in the Bible?

16. What is the shortest book in the Bible?

17. What is the longest chapter in the Bible?

18. What is the shortest chapter in the Bible?

19. What is the longest verse in the Bible?

20. What is the shortest verse in the Bible?

21. The first five books of the Bible are called the
    a) Fantastic Five
    b) Pentagon
    c) Pomegranate
    d) Pentateuch

22. Who wrote the first five books of the Bible?

23. The first event in the Old Testament is the
    a) creation of the universe
    b) creation of the first marshmallows
    c) great flood
    d) birth of Jesus

24. In the Old Testament, the nation of Israel was divided into how many tribes?

25. Fill in the missing tribes of Israel: Judah, Issachar, Zebulun, Reuben, Simeon, _____, Ephraim, Manasseh, Benjamin, ____, Asher, ____ (Numbers 2:3-31).

26. The Law in the Pentateuch is often called the Mosaic Law because
   a) God gave the laws to Moses
   b) all the laws are different, creating a "mosaic" of instructions
   c) Moses broke the stone tablets and made up his own law
   d) Moses liked mosaic art

27. Why are there so many names listed in several of the early Old Testament books?

28. True or False: We know who wrote all the books of the Old Testament.

29. The number of years between the end of the Old Testament and the beginning of the New Testament is
   a) zero
   b) four hundred
   c) one thousand
   d) not known

30. True or False: When the New Testament was written, Israel was the largest and most powerful nation on earth.

31. Name the first four books of the New Testament, which are also known as the four Gospels.

32. The four Gospels tell about
a) the life and ministry of Jesus
b) Noah's ark
c) Paul's mission work
d) the invention of the first toys

33. True or False: Christians only need to read the four Gospels.

34. In the four Gospels, we can find
a) stories Jesus told
b) Jesus' family lineage
c) accounts of Jesus' resurrection
d) all of the above

35. What does *epistle* mean?
a) a part of a flower
b) a type of gun
c) a letter
d) a kind of glitter

36. What is a Gentile?

37. The first missionary to the Gentiles was
a) Larry the Cucumber
b) Billy Graham
c) Paul the apostle
d) John the Baptist

38. Fill in the blank: We can read about the travels of the first missionary to the Gentiles in the book of

_____.

39. Paul the apostle wrote many letters that are included in the New Testament. They give Christians instructions on how to

    a) get revenge on the Romans

    b) garden

    c) love one another, behave, and conduct church business

    d) make cinnamon rolls

40. Why are these letters important to Christians today?

41. Throughout Paul's letters, he says Christians must have

    a) love

    b) husbands or wives

    c) riches

    d) flip-flops

42. True or False: The books of James, 1 and 2 Peter, 1, 2, and 3 John, and Jude are all named after the people who wrote them.

43. What is the last book of the New Testament?

CREATION

44. Where is the account of creation found in the Bible?

45. When did God create "the heaven and the earth"?

46. How many days of creation were there?
a) one
b) ten
c) six
d) seven

47. What did God allow Adam and Eve to eat?
a) seed-bearing plants and fruit
b) grasses
c) sprinkles
d) sushi

48. How did God describe "everything that he had made"?

49. Fill in the blank: God said, "It is not good for the man to be _____. I will make a helper suitable for him."

50. Put the following list in creation chronological order:
___animals and man
___light
___sun and moon and stars
___skies and seas
___rest
___plants and flowers and trees
___birds and fish

51. Who wrote the book of Genesis?

52. What did God do on the first day?

53. What three things did God create on the fourth day to light the universe?

54. **FUNTASTIC FACT!** Gold and onyx could be found in the garden of Eden (Genesis 2:12).

55. Why did Eden have a river running through it?
    a) to swim in
    b) to bathe in
    c) to water the garden
    d) to do laundry in

56. The name of the first man was
    a) Douglas
    b) Noah
    c) Buford
    d) Adam

57. Who named all the living creatures?

58. The name of the first woman was
    a) Penelope
    b) Crystal
    c) Eve
    d) Rebekah

59. **FUNTASTIC FACT!** The first woman's name meant "mother of all living" (Genesis 3:20 KJV).

60. What did God take from Adam to make Eve?

61. FUNTASTIC FACT! Adam and Eve were the first married couple (Genesis 2:23–24).

62. The first woman was tempted by a
    a) dinosaur
    b) unicorn
    c) serpent
    d) spider

63. If Eve would eat the forbidden fruit, the serpent promised her
    a) a new car
    b) riches
    c) a starring role in a movie
    d) knowledge of good and evil

64. After discovering their nakedness, how did Adam and Eve clothe themselves?

65. What did Adam and Eve do when they heard God calling?

66. When he was caught disobeying God, Adam blamed
    a) the serpent
    b) bad TV shows
    c) Cain
    d) Eve

67. After Adam and Eve ate the forbidden fruit, God
    a) sent them out of Eden
    b) let them stay in Eden
    c) poured manna from heaven
    d) told them to build an ark so He could begin the human race again

68. Whom did God put in place to guard the tree of life?
   a) Batman
   b) Superman
   c) cherubim
   d) a ninja

69. Where was the forbidden tree located in the garden?

70. What was the name of the forbidden tree?

71. What tree stood near the forbidden tree?

72. How many rivers were in the garden of Eden?

73. When God cursed the ground, what did He say it would bring forth?
   a) mushrooms
   b) squash
   c) eggplant
   d) thorns and thistles

74. What job was given to cherubim after the expulsion of Adam and Eve from Eden?

NOAH AND THE GREAT FLOOD

75. You can learn about Noah's ark in the book of
   a) Genesis
   b) Revelation
   c) Bubbles
   d) Noah

76. True or False: In Noah's time, God was pleased with His creation.

77. Noah was known as what kind of man?
   a) funny
   b) obnoxious
   c) righteous
   d) athletic

78. Can you name Noah's sons? (Hint: One of them has the same name as a favorite lunch meat.)

79. How many years did Noah spend preparing the ark as God told him?
   a) ten
   b) fifty
   c) seventy-five
   d) one hundred

80. What kind of wood did Noah build the ark out of?
   a) oak
   b) Christmas tree
   c) gopher wood
   d) cedar

81. **FUNTASTIC FACT!** God told Noah to take *seven pairs* of each type of bird with him into the ark (Genesis 7:3). He also told Noah to take one pair of each ritually unclean animal and seven pairs of each ritually clean animal (Genesis 7:2).

82. **When the flood started, Noah was**
    a) 6 years old
    b) 60 years old
    c) 600 years old
    d) 666 years old

83. **Fill in the blank: "Noah found _____ in the eyes of the Lord."**

84. **How long did it rain?**

85. **FUNTASTIC FACT!** The great floodwater rose until it was about twenty-five feet over the highest mountains (Genesis 7:20).

86. **Noah could see the mountaintops after**
    a) seven and a half months
    b) ten months
    c) seven days
    d) forty days and forty nights

87. **Fill in the blank: The first bird Noah sent out from the ark was a _____.**

88. **The next bird Noah sent out from the ark was**
    a) another raven
    b) a flamingo
    c) a penguin
    d) a dove

89. After the second time out, the dove brought Noah
    a) a nest
    b) a garlic clove
    c) a water bottle
    d) an olive branch

90. After God saved Noah's family from the flood, Noah
    a) cut his hair
    b) made a golden calf
    c) built an altar to God and made sacrifices upon it
    d) made smoothies for everyone

91. After the flood, the Bible says that Noah
    a) ran a marathon
    b) planted a vineyard
    c) bred goats and sheep
    d) never looked at water again

92. True or False: God promised not to destroy the earth by flood again.

93. What do we often see in the sky after rainfall that reminds us of God's promise to Noah?

94. How old was Noah when he died?
    a) 650
    b) 750
    c) 850
    d) 950

TOWER OF BABEL

95. FUNTASTIC FACT! Nimrod built the city of Babel, which later became Babylon and the city of Nineveh (Genesis 10:8–11).

96. True or False: When the people first started building the Tower of Babel, they all spoke the same language.

97. The people who built the tower spoke
- a) Latin
- b) Hebrew
- c) Spanish
- d) an unspecified language

98. The tower was built of
- a) Legos
- b) stone
- c) brick
- d) Play-Doh

99. True or False: The people were building a city as well as a tower.

100. The people wanted a tower that would
- a) make a good fort for snowball fights
- b) be three feet taller than the Empire State Building
- c) make a good home for Rapunzel
- d) reach to heaven

101. True or False: God was happy when He saw the tower.

102. When He saw the tower, God
    a) gave the people a golden calf
    b) kicked it down
    c) built it higher
    d) made the people all speak different languages
       so they couldn't finish the work

103. Why is the story of the Tower of Babel important?

GOD'S PROMISE TO ABRAHAM

104. True or False: The story of Abraham is found in the book of Genesis.

105. In which chapter can you find the story of God's promise to Abraham?

106. True or False: Abraham was named Abram before God changed his name.

107. How old was Abraham when God appeared to him?
    a) one
    b) ten
    c) ninety-nine
    d) one hundred

108. God told Abraham to
    a) build an ark
    b) make Him a PB&J
    c) obey Him
    d) name all the animals

109. When Abraham saw God, he
    a) told God he was afraid
    b) bowed down, touching his face to the ground
    c) built an altar
    d) screamed in excitement

110. FUNTASTIC FACT! God wanted to make a covenant with Abraham. A covenant is a solemn promise.

111. True or False: God promised Abraham that he would have many descendants.

112. A descendant is
    a) a relative of a future generation
    b) an ancestor
    c) a person walking down a staircase
    d) an airplane going down in the sky

113. God also promised Abraham
    a) a new yo-yo
    b) a fruit basket
    c) a coat of many colors
    d) the land of Canaan

114. True or False: God plans for His covenant with Abraham to last forever.

115. God gave Abram the name Abraham because
- a) it fit better in the song "Father Abraham"
- b) it was easier to spell
- c) Abraham was to be the father of many nations
- d) He wanted to name him after Abraham Lincoln

116. True or False: God said that some of Abraham's descendants would be kings.

117. True or False: As part of the covenant, God wanted Abraham and his descendants to worship Him.

118. God changed the name of Abraham's wife. Do you remember what Sarah's name was before God changed it?

119. God promised Sarah she would
- a) never have to work again
- b) have a lifetime supply of coffee
- c) have a baby
- d) get a new puppy

120. When God promised Abraham that his wife Sarah would have a baby, Abraham
- a) bowed down to God
- b) laughed
- c) sang God a psalm
- d) did a happy dance

121. Which did God promise Sarah—a baby boy or a baby girl?

122. Abraham was surprised by God's promise because Sarah
- a) had vowed never to have children
- b) was CEO of a large company and had no time for kids
- c) was ninety years old, which is usually too old to have a baby
- d) already had thirteen boys

123. How old was Abraham when God promised him that Sarah would bear a baby?

124. An heir is
- a) a person with too much hair
- b) an honest mistake
- c) a person who receives an inheritance
- d) an airhead

125. True or False: God agreed with Abraham that Ishmael should be Abraham's heir.

126. How do you think Abraham's covenant with God affects you today?

JACOB AND ESAU

127. FUNTASTIC FACT! You can find the account of Jacob and Esau in Genesis, chapters 25–36.

128. The Bible says that Esau sold Jacob his birthright because he thought
   a) Jacob was entitled to it
   b) he would die from hunger and would have no use for it
   c) he wanted to buy new toys
   d) Jacob would eventually return his rights to him

129. What did Jacob use to purchase Esau's birthright?

130. What did Jacob wear to make his father, whose eyes were dim with age, think he was hairy like Esau?

131. God promised Jacob that
   a) he would be the father of kings
   b) all who hated him would be cursed
   c) he would have a lifetime supply of jelly
   d) he would be greater than Abraham

132. True or False: Jacob was renamed Israel.

133. Who was Esau's mother?

134. Esau liked to
   a) fish
   b) jump rope
   c) study the Torah
   d) hunt

135. Jacob called himself Esau's
   a) servant
   b) master
   c) brother
   d) BFF

PLAGUES ON EGYPT

136. **FUNTASTIC FACT!** God sent plagues on Egypt so that the Egyptians would know that He is Lord (Exodus 7–12).

137. Put the plagues in the order in which they occurred:
__boils
__darkness
__water to blood
__locusts
__death of firstborn
__frogs
__diseased livestock
__flies
__hail and fire
__lice

138. When the water turned to blood, what happened to the fish in the river?

139. How many days passed between the first and second plagues?

140. How many of the plagues did Pharaoh's magicians duplicate?

141. Fill in the blank: God told Aaron to stretch out his rod so that the dust of the land would become _____.

142. How long did darkness cover the land?

143. True or False: When darkness covered the land, the children of Israel had light.

144. Which part of Egypt was set apart so that the swarms of flies didn't go there?

145. What did God tell Moses to scatter to cause boils on the Egyptians?

146. Why does the Bible say that Pharaoh's magicians could not stand before Moses?
    a) they couldn't see in the darkness
    b) they were ashamed
    c) they were covered in boils
    d) they couldn't get through the swarms of flies

147. Where did the wind blow the locusts?

THE TEN COMMANDMENTS

148. **FUNTASTIC FACT!** The Ten Commandments appear in the Bible twice. You can find them in Exodus 20:1-17 and Deuteronomy 5:1-21.

Fill in the blanks:

149. In the first commandment, God said, "You shall have no other _____ before me."

150. In the second commandment, God said, "You shall not make for yourself a carved _____, or any likeness of anything that is in heaven above, or that is in the earth beneath, or that is in the water under the earth."

151. In the third commandment, God said, "You shall not take the name of the LORD your God in_____."

152. In the fourth commandment, God said, "Remember the Sabbath day, to keep it _____."

153. In the fifth commandment, God said, "Honor your _____ and your _____."

154. In the sixth commandment, God said, "You shall not _____."

155. In the seventh commandment, God said, "You shall not commit _____."

156. In the eighth commandment, God said, "You shall not _____."

157. In the ninth commandment, God said, "You shall not bear false _____ against your neighbor."

158. In the tenth commandment, God said, "You shall not _____."

159. God also gave Moses other laws. Most of them can be found in the book of
    a) Leviticus
    b) Numbers
    c) Acts
    d) Revelation

160. When God issued the Ten Commandments, He was on
   a) the banks of the River Jordan
   b) Mount Sinai
   c) a boat
   d) Mount Everest

161. When God gave them the Ten Commandments, the Israelites had just
   a) built a city
   b) been brought out of slavery in Egypt
   c) discovered electricity
   d) finished watching *Star Wars*

162. The Lord wrote the Ten Commandments on
   a) sheepskin
   b) stone tablets
   c) an iPad
   d) Thursday

163. FUNTASTIC FACT! *Exodus* means "departure."

164. True or False: It is okay to worship statues, money, and other earthly goods as long as we attend church every Sunday.

165. What does God mean when He says not to take His name "in vain"?

166. God commands us to set aside one day a week to
   a) mow the lawn
   b) read the Bible and only drink water all day
   c) watch TV
   d) keep holy, cease work, and remember His people's deliverance from Egypt

167. Why did God say He wanted us to rest every seventh day?

168. God's commandment not to commit adultery shows us how much God values marriage. Where does God establish the institution of marriage?

169. God tells us not to covet other people's possessions. That means we should not
    a) steal from our friends
    b) destroy other people's belongings
    c) make fun of others
    d) wish we had our neighbor's stuff

170. True or False: The original copy of the Ten Commandments is on display at the Jerusalem Museum.

171. FUNTASTIC FACT! Jesus said, "Do not think that I have come to abolish the Law or the Prophets; I have not come to abolish them but to fulfill them" (Matthew 5:17 ESV).

ARK OF THE COVENANT

172. FUNTASTIC FACT! At Beth Shemesh, 50,070 men died because they looked into the ark of the covenant (1 Samuel 6:19 NKJV).

173. What was the ark of the covenant?

174. What covered the poles that were used to carry the ark of the covenant?

175. True or False: The ark of the covenant was made after the death of Moses.

176. Fill in the blank: "At that time the LORD set apart the tribe of _____ to carry the ark of the covenant of the LORD."

177. What was Eli's reaction when he learned his two sons had been killed and the ark captured by the enemy?

178. While the ark was being moved, what caused Uzzah to touch it in an attempt to right it, resulting in his death?
    a) a strong east wind blew and upset it
    b) oxen pulling the cart carrying it stumbled
    c) the men holding it by poles through the rings
        stumbled
    d) Uzzah replaced the lid, which had slipped off

179. Who built a temple for the ark?
    a) Absalom
    b) David
    c) Herod the Great
    d) Solomon

180. When in the tabernacle (tent), the ark was in an area called what?

181. According to the book of Hebrews, the ark contained a gold jar of manna, the stone tablets of the covenant, and what third item?
- a) the bronze snake Moses had put on a pole that the people looked at and lived
- b) a tribute of gold given by the enemies of Israel when they returned the ark
- c) Aaron's staff that had budded
- d) the books of the law of Moses

182. Where will the ark of the covenant ultimately be found?

183. Who was the last person on earth to see the ark of the covenant?

184. On what mountain was the ark of the covenant built?
- a) Everest
- b) Sinai
- c) Olympus
- d) Kilimanjaro

JOSHUA'S FAMOUS BATTLE

185. FUNTASTIC FACT! God said the Israelites should never become discouraged because He would be with them wherever they went (Joshua 1:9).

186. True or False: Moses was led by God to appoint Joshua to be his successor.

187. The book of Joshua begins recording what happened right after
   a) the Israelites went white-water rafting on the Jordan River
   b) the great flood
   c) the death of Moses
   d) the birth of Jesus

188. Who wrote the book of Joshua?

189. God told Joshua to take the people of Israel to the land He had promised them, located across the
   a) Red Sea
   b) Grand Canyon
   c) Jordan River
   d) Nile River

190. Joshua's spies in Jericho stayed at
   a) a bed-and-breakfast
   b) a Pharisee's house
   c) the home of a wicked woman
   d) Mary Magdalene's house

191. True or False: Rahab protected the spies from the men of Jericho.

192. FUNTASTIC FACT! No one could leave or enter a city after the gate was closed at sundown. Rahab tricked the men who were chasing Joshua's spies and told them to look outside the city. Because the men were locked out after sundown, they could not harm the spies (Joshua 2:4–7).

193. Rahab hid the spies
   a) on the roof
   b) under the table
   c) in the bathtub
   d) under her bed

194. FUNTASTIC FACT! In addition to protecting them, Rahab gave the spies valuable information. She told them that the people of Jericho were afraid of the Israelites. This gave the spies confidence that the Lord would help them conquer Jericho (Joshua 2:9, 24).

195. True or False: Rahab accepted the Lord and asked the spies for mercy.

196. Why did Rahab protect the spies?

197. FUNTASTIC FACT! God stopped the Jordan River from flowing while the Israelites crossed it into the Promised Land. The river was usually flooded at that time of year, so crossing it on foot would have been impossible without God's miracle. The stopping of the river also allowed the ark of the covenant to stay dry while the priests carried it (Joshua 3:14–17).

198. How many men crossed the plains of Jericho to fight for the Lord?

199. The Israelites no longer had manna to eat after they had
   a) been punished for watching too much TV
   b) eaten food grown in the Promised Land
   c) gotten tired of eating salmon
   d) eaten brussels sprouts

200. What was manna?

201. True or False: The walls of Jericho came tumbling down after the Israelites threw rocks and stones at them.

202. Whose family was spared during the fall of Jericho?

203. All the silver, gold, bronze, and iron in Jericho was
    a) used to improve the ark of the covenant
    b) put into the Lord's treasury
    c) used to build the Tower of Babel
    d) made into fancy jewelry

204. True or False: After the fall of Jericho, Joshua became famous in the land.

A JUDGE NAMED DEBORAH

205. Where in the Old Testament can we find out about the judges of Israel?

206. FUNTASTIC FACT! The name Deborah means "hornet."

207. True or False: Women judges were common in the Old Testament.

208. Deborah was also a
    a) florist
    b) fashion designer
    c) baker
    d) prophet

209. True or False: In Deborah's time, Israel was a free nation.

210. King Jabin of Canaan
    a) made life very hard for the Israelites
    b) promised to feed his subjects tacos
    c) forced the Israelites to worship gold statues
       of himself
    d) built cities out of Legos

211. How many iron chariots did King Jabin have?

212. How many years did the Israelites live under King Jabin's rule before they asked God for help?

213. Why was God punishing Israel at this time?

214. True or False: After the people cried out for help, the Lord told Deborah what to do to deliver her people.

215. Deborah planned to
    a) poison the enemy's water supply
    b) pray for a plague of frogs to torture the enemy
    c) deliver the enemy into the hands of Israel's
       general
    d) burn down the enemy's tents

216. The enemy was to be defeated at Mount Tabor. Where was Mount Tabor located?

217. Barak was
   a) a famous chef
   b) a landscaper
   c) a general in Israel's army
   d) Deborah's husband

218. Rather than confront the enemy alone, Barak wanted to take along
   a) Deborah, to ensure success
   b) a smartphone
   c) a pit bull
   d) ten thousand men, to outnumber the king's army

219. Deborah agreed but said the credit for the victory would go to
   a) Barak
   b) a woman
   c) Pizza Hut, for providing the army with food
   d) the army's corporate sponsors

220. True or False: In Old Testament times, it was customary for women in Israel to lead battles because in that nation they were considered superior to men.

221. Did God give the Israelites complete victory over Sisera's army?

222. You can read a poem about the battle in
   a) the fifth chapter of Judges
   b) the first chapter of Genesis
   c) *Where the Sidewalk Ends* by Shel Silverstein
   d) the Psalms

223. After the people of Israel cried out to God for help, He answered their prayers. When was the last time you prayed to God for help? What happened?

SAMSON
◇◇◇◇◇◇◇◇◇◇◇◇◇

224. Samson's story is found in what book of the Bible?

225. True or False: Samson's parents were pleased by his marriage to a Philistine woman.

226. Samson killed a lion with
   a) his bare hands
   b) a slingshot
   c) a sword
   d) a Nerf gun

227. After Samson killed the lion, he later found what edible substance inside its carcass?

228. To avenge himself over the loss of his wife, Samson
   a) made the Philistines his slaves
   b) burned the Philistines' corn
   c) destroyed the statue of the Philistine god Dagon
   d) killed the Philistine king with a sword

229. What happened when the Jews bound Samson as punishment, planning to turn him over to the Philistines?

230. True or False: Samson killed one thousand Philistines with his bare hands.

231. When enemies tried to kill Samson in Gaza, he
    a) blew a horn until the city walls fell
    b) killed the enemies with his lightsaber
    c) took Delilah hostage
    d) carried away the city gate

232. What secret of Samson's were his enemies eager to discover?

233. True or False: The enemies bribed Samson's girlfriend, Delilah, with 1,100 pieces of silver each to tell them Samson's secret.

234. Fill in the blanks: "A _____ has never come upon my head, for I have been a Nazirite to God from my mother's womb. If my head is _____, then my strength will leave me, and I shall become weak and be like any other man."

235. True or False: Samson's capture caused the Philistines to praise Jehovah.

236. Fill in the blank: "Then Samson called to the LORD and said, 'O LORD GOD, please remember me and please _____me only this once, O God, that I may be avenged on the Philistines for my two eyes.'"

237. In order to kill three thousand Philistines, Samson
   a) destroyed the pillars of a crowded house,
      causing its collapse
   b) enlisted the help of the Israelite army
   c) turned his staff into many poisonous serpents
      that bit them
   d) picked up the city gate and swung it at them

238. True or False: Samson prayed to die along with
the Philistines.

RUTH AND BOAZ

239. **FUNTASTIC FACT!** The only other Boaz mentioned
in the Bible was a pillar in front of the temple. Boaz's
great-great-grandson Solomon named that pillar
(1 Kings 7:21).

240. The events in the book of Ruth take place when
what group of people ruled Israel?
   a) judges
   b) priests
   c) kings
   d) pharaohs

241. How many people of Naomi's family went to
Moab?

242. From what city was Naomi's family?

243. True or False: Naomi's sons were already
married when her husband died.

244. What were the names of Naomi's sons?

245. Naomi told her daughters-in-law to stay in Moab after her sons died because
    a) there was still famine in Israel
    b) the road to Israel was unsafe for beautiful young women to travel
    c) she couldn't bear more sons for them to marry
    d) the Israelites wouldn't accept them

246. After Naomi returned to her home, she told people to call her
    a) Mara, meaning "bitter"
    b) Rachel, meaning "ewe"
    c) Salome, meaning "peace"
    d) Edna, meaning "reborn"

247. What grain was being harvested when Naomi and Ruth returned to Bethlehem?

248. True or False: At first, Boaz was angry at Ruth for gleaning because he was worried that his men would pester the beautiful young woman.

249. True or False: Naomi told Ruth to provide a banquet for Boaz.

250. When Naomi gave her instructions on how to endear herself to Boaz, Ruth
    a) protested that Boaz was too old for her
    b) said he was not her nearest relative
    c) said she would do as Naomi instructed
    d) had to be convinced since she had attracted the attention of many men

251. True or False: Boaz immediately proposed marriage to Ruth.

252. When the nearest kinsman gave up his right to the family property, he
    a) called Boaz a thief
    b) vowed revenge
    c) took off his shoe
    d) all of the above

253. The townswomen said Ruth was more valuable to Naomi than
    a) seven sons
    b) half the kingdom
    c) seven sons and seven daughters
    d) thirty gold talents

254. After she and Boaz married, Ruth gave birth to a son, Obed. Why is this important?

DAVID FIGHTS GOLIATH

255. Why did David visit the Israelites' battlefield?
    a) he got out of school early
    b) he was taking food to his brothers
    c) he was looking for the golf ball he lost
    d) he was chasing a sheep

256. FUNTASTIC FACT! Goliath of Gath was over nine feet tall (1 Samuel 17:4)!

257. True or False: Goliath was never heavily armed. He depended on his size to protect him.

258. True or False: When Goliath challenged the Israelites to send a man to fight him, many men eagerly volunteered.

259. Before he met Goliath, David
    a) was next in line to be a high priest
    b) tended sheep
    c) was a prince of Israel
    d) learned to fight giants by jousting with a cousin

260. True or False: While David was visiting his brothers on the battlefield, Goliath challenged the Israelites.

261. FUNTASTIC FACT! King Saul had promised a reward to the person who killed Goliath. In addition to money, King Saul promised his daughter in marriage, and the victor's father's family would not have to pay taxes (1 Samuel 17:25).

262. True or False: David's brothers were sure David could easily slay Goliath.

263. When David heard the giant's challenge, he
    a) wondered how Goliath dared to defy the army of the living God
    b) became scared and ran home
    c) took a selfie with Goliath
    d) threatened to take Goliath to court

264. How many days did Goliath taunt the Israelites?

265. Saul did not want David to fight Goliath because David
    a) already had plans at a friend's house
    b) was a consultant to King Saul
    c) was only a boy
    d) was an old man

266. FUNTASTIC FACT! King Saul gave David his own bronze helmet and coat of armor to use when fighting Goliath (1 Samuel 17:38).

267. True or False: David convinced King Saul to let him fight Goliath by telling him that God had protected David from the lions and bears that attacked his sheep.

268. David took Saul's armor off because
    a) the color clashed with his dark hair
    b) it was too old-fashioned
    c) he couldn't walk in it because he wasn't used to such bulky armor
    d) his friends would make fun of him

269. How many smooth stones did David pick up to battle Goliath?

270. True or False: When Goliath saw David coming to battle him, he shook with fear.

271. David told Goliath that his victory over him would prove that
   a) dogs rule and cats drool
   b) he had been paying attention when he watched *Star Wars*
   c) size means nothing
   d) there is a God in Israel

272. True or False: Goliath fell with the first stone David hurled at him.

273. After Goliath died, the Israelites
   a) chased the Philistines back to their own country
   b) offered the Philistines a permanent peace treaty
   c) slept
   d) went to the beach to relax

A VISIT FROM THE QUEEN

274. Can you find the story of the queen's visit to Solomon in the Old Testament or the New Testament?

275. The queen was from
   a) Australia
   b) France
   c) Babylon
   d) Sheba

276. The queen visited King Solomon because
   a) she had heard of his fame
   b) she was looking for a husband
   c) she was hungry and heard he served great
      food
   d) he had the best video game arcade in all of
      Israel

277. FUNTASTIC FACT! According to Bible scholars, the queen's country was located about 1,200 miles from Jerusalem. Although airplanes make traveling such distances easy today, the queen had to go by camel or horseback, making the trip long and difficult.

278. True or False: The queen wanted to test Solomon with difficult questions.

279. The queen's first question was
   a) "Why did the chicken cross the road?"
   b) "What's your favorite color?"
   c) "Why are you so wise?"
   d) unknown; her questions are not recorded in
      the Bible

280. The queen was amazed by Solomon's
   a) wisdom and sacrifices to God
   b) hairstyle
   c) ability to recite the entire Bible from memory
   d) skills at video games

281. The queen was also amazed by Solomon's
   a) willingness to live a life of poverty
   b) horses
   c) riches, palace, food, and servants
   d) ability to read her mind and perform magic
      tricks

282. True or False: The queen told Solomon she was disappointed that he didn't know as much as she had been told.

283. True or False: After she had spoken with Solomon, the queen praised the Lord.

284. If the queen did praise God, why would this be important?

285. FUNTASTIC FACT! The queen gave Solomon 120 talents of gold and many spices and jewels (1 Kings 10:10; 2 Chronicles 9:9).

286. If one talent weighs seventy-five pounds, how many pounds of gold did the queen of Sheba give to Solomon?

ELIJAH AND ELISHA

287. We first meet Elijah in
    a) 1 Kings
    b) Genesis
    c) Acts
    d) study hall

288. Elijah was
    a) a doctor
    b) a policeman
    c) a prophet
    d) the writer of the Gospel of John

289. True or False: Elijah served the Lord of Israel.

290. Elijah told King Ahab that there would be
    a) pizza for supper every day
    b) seven years of bounty, followed by seven
       years of famine
    c) a great ship named *Titanic* that would sink on
       her maiden voyage
    d) no rain for the next few years until God
       commanded rain to fall

291. Why do you think God told Elijah to give King Ahab this message?

292. True or False: King Ahab was a godly king who loved the Lord.

293. King Ahab
    a) honored the God of Israel with sacrifices
       pleasing to Him
    b) worshipped the god Baal
    c) went on TV to proclaim God's greatness
    d) was the best king Israel ever had

294. God told Elijah to hide because
    a) Elijah's prophecy had made King Ahab mad
    b) he was famous and God wanted him to avoid
       photographers
    c) King Ahab wanted to honor him with food
       forbidden to Jews
    d) hide-and-seek was the favorite game of King
       Ahab's small son

295. While he was hiding, Elijah's food would be brought to him by
   a) ravens
   b) doves
   c) the pizza delivery guy
   d) an ice cream truck, since the ravine was on its route

296. Elijah's food consisted of
   a) cheeseburgers in the morning and mac and cheese in the evening
   b) pancakes in the morning and ham and waffles in the evening
   c) any food his heart desired
   d) bread and meat in the morning and evening

297. After the brook dried up, Elijah was fed by
   a) bigger, better ravens
   b) a widow
   c) locusts
   d) John the Baptist

298. Why did the brook dry up?

299. True or False: The widow who fed Elijah after the brook dried up had plenty of rich food to eat.

300. After the widow's son died, Elijah
   a) told her she shouldn't have let him ride that roller coaster
   b) gave her herbs and green tea
   c) said she should have called 911 sooner
   d) prayed to God

301. True or False: The widow's son rose from the dead.

302. Elijah physically revived the widow's son by doing what?
   a) breathing on him
   b) stretching himself out on the boy three times
   c) reading to him
   d) anointing him with oil

303. What did Elijah use to make his altar on Mount Carmel?

304. Elijah killed 450 prophets of what god?

305. True or False: When Elijah was standing on the mountain, God spoke to him out of an earthquake.

306. Some people said Jesus was
   a) Elijah
   b) John the Baptist
   c) Jeremiah
   d) all of the above

307. True or False: Jesus spoke to Moses and Elijah before He was crucified.

308. Why would the Jews be looking for Elijah to come back from the dead?

309. True or False: Jesus said Elijah had returned.

310. FUNTASTIC FACT! Elijah was taken to heaven by a chariot of fire (2 Kings 2:11).

311. Elijah was taken up to heaven in a weather anomaly known as a what?
- a) whirlwind
- b) thunderbolt
- c) waterspout
- d) tsunami

312. When Elisha succeeded Elijah, what did he receive of Elijah's as a symbol of his succession?
- a) a cloak
- b) a rod
- c) a ring
- d) a robe

313. True or False: Elisha was the son of the prophet Elijah.

314. You can find out about Elisha in
- a) 1 Kings
- b) 2 Kings
- c) Matthew
- d) Revelation

315. True or False: Elisha was married.

316. True or False: Elisha asked for a "double portion" of Elijah's spirit.

317. Elisha's first miracle was
- a) making five thousand sandwiches from one can of Spam
- b) dividing the Jordan River and walking on dry land
- c) inventing the lightbulb
- d) getting the children of Jericho to eat sushi

318. True or False: The fifty prophets of Jericho saw the miracle and proclaimed that Elijah's power was upon Elisha.

319. In Jericho, Elisha
    a) opened a candy factory
    b) gave a bowl of spinach to every child he met
    c) made the water pure
    d) turned water into wine

320. Some boys in Bethel made fun of Elisha for being
    a) handsome
    b) short
    c) bald
    d) a nerd

321. When some young people mocked Elisha by calling him "bald head," what animals did God send to punish them?
    a) lions
    b) bears
    c) wolves
    d) a & c

322. The Moabites had
    a) poisoned the Jordan River
    b) turned the Nile River red
    c) rebelled against Israel
    d) robbed the bank

323. True or False: Elisha told the kings to build ditches in a dry stream bed.

324. The next day, the Moabites decided to loot the Israelites' camp because
   a) Elisha told them to
   b) Jezebel rose from the dead and promised victory
   c) they thought the water they saw around the camp was blood
   d) they had promised to bring their girlfriends some jewelry

325. What happened when the Moabites reached the Israelites' camp?

326. True or False: The Israelites conquered all of Moab until only the capital city of Kir-haraseth was left.

327. Later, a widow asked Elisha for help because she
   a) was in debt
   b) wanted to be beautiful
   c) wanted to find another husband
   d) needed a new roof on her house

328. The only item the widow had in her house was
   a) a small coin
   b) a broom
   c) a single rose
   d) a small jar of olive oil

329. Describe the miracle that happened when the widow followed Elisha's instructions.

330. When a prophet's widow needed money to save her sons, Elisha multiplied her last pot of
    a) oil
    b) corn
    c) meal
    d) wheat

331. True or False: Because of Elisha's advice, the widow had enough money to pay off her debts, with enough left over to live on.

332. Elisha offered to put in a good word with the king for a rich woman who had been kind to him. Did she accept his offer?

333. Elisha rewarded the Shunammite woman's kindness by
    a) praising her to the king
    b) promising her that she would have a baby
    c) giving her permission to charge tolls to people entering Jerusalem
    d) giving her free Wi-Fi for a year

334. The kindness that the woman had done for Elisha was
    a) giving him water at the well
    b) buying him tickets to an amusement park
    c) setting up a room for him to stay in when he visited
    d) washing his feet with expensive perfume

335. True or False: Years later, Elisha performed a miracle for the woman's son.

336. Elisha
  a) brought the boy back from the dead
  b) refused to perform a miracle
  c) healed the boy's blindness
  d) gave the boy wisdom so he could pass his
     college entrance exams

337. FUNTASTIC FACT! Elisha fed one hundred men with twenty loaves of bread. Even though this normally would not have been enough food for so many, they all feasted and had food left over (2 Kings 4:42–44).

338. True or False: Elisha purified a pot of stew that contained poisonous gourds.

339. True or False: Naaman was a respected Egyptian commander.

340. Naaman suffered from
  a) leprosy
  b) the flu
  c) chicken pox
  d) debt

341. Who suggested that Elisha could cure Naaman?

342. True or False: Elisha was not afraid to try to heal Naaman. He told the king that he would prove Israel had a prophet.

343. Elisha sent his servant to tell Naaman to
  a) wash seven times in the Jordan River
  b) eat more chicken
  c) sit on a stump and sing silly songs
  d) go on a long journey

344. When Naaman was told what he should do to get well, he
   a) cried
   b) was angry
   c) was eager to proceed
   d) decided to kill Elisha

345. True or False: Elisha's instructions caused Naaman to become even more sick.

346. After Naaman was cured, whom did he vow to worship?

347. The amount of soil Naaman took with him was
   a) a jarful
   b) a bushel
   c) a ton
   d) two mule loads

348. FUNTASTIC FACT! Elisha refused to accept any payment in return for curing Naaman (2 Kings 5:16).

349. Elisha's devious servant was named what?
   a) Hobson
   b) Gehazi
   c) Ziba
   d) Zimri

350. True or False: Elisha's servant ran after Naaman and asked him for money and clothes.

351. Did Naaman give the servant any gifts?

352. True or False: Elisha was happy with the servant's actions.

353. When he heard what Gehazi had done, Elisha
   a) rewarded him with half the money
   b) complimented Gehazi on how smart he was
   c) gave him a bigger Christmas bonus than usual
   d) said that Gehazi and his family would always
      be plagued with leprosy

A WICKED KING

354. True or False: All the kings of Israel during the time of the book of 1 Kings were good.

355. FUNTASTIC FACT! King Ahab ruled Israel from 874 to 853 BC. This was over eight hundred years before Jesus was born.

356. King Ahab
   a) loved the God of Israel
   b) worshipped the god Baal
   c) promised the people new high schools
   d) sponsored free concerts at the mall

357. King Ahab's wife was named
   a) Mary Margaret
   b) Jezebel
   c) Belle
   d) Cruella

358. True or False: After King Ahab married, he rededicated his life to the God of Israel.

359. True or False: Ahab angered God more than any king of Israel before him.

360. God sent Elijah the prophet to tell Ahab there would be a drought until
- a) Ahab changed his ways
- b) Ahab sacrificed a lamb, two rams, and three doves
- c) God commanded it to rain
- d) spring break

361. True or False: God sent His prophet Elijah to tell Ahab's people not to follow Baal.

362. King Ahab wanted the vineyard of Naboth the Jezreelite because
- a) it was near his palace and he wanted to use it as a vegetable garden
- b) it was a perfect location to film a movie
- c) he needed the land so he could build a temple to Baal
- d) his goats needed more land for pasture

363. In return for the vineyard, King Ahab promised Naboth
- a) a better vineyard or to pay him what it was worth
- b) a lifetime supply of doughnuts
- c) blessings from Baal
- d) season tickets for his favorite baseball team

364. Naboth refused to let King Ahab have the vineyard because

    a) he had lost the deed to the land in a Monopoly game

    b) the land belonged to his mother-in-law

    c) the land was not good enough for the glorious King Ahab

    d) God refused to let him give King Ahab the land

365. After Naboth refused to give Ahab the land, the king

    a) threw his video games at the TV

    b) stamped his feet, shook his fists, and cried

    c) sulked and refused to eat

    d) prayed to Baal to curse Naboth

366. True or False: After seeing her husband's anger, Ahab's wife plotted to kill Naboth.

367. Did Ahab's wife get revenge on Naboth?

368. When Naboth's vineyard became available, King Ahab

    a) took it

    b) celebrated by playing the ukulele

    c) paid Naboth's family ten times what the land was worth

    d) toilet papered it

369. True or False: The God of Israel was not fooled by Jezebel's clever plan of revenge on Naboth.

370. Who gave King Ahab the message from God that Ahab would pay for his sin?

371. True or False: Ahab's punishment from the Lord was death.

372. Like Ahab, which king built up a grove for the worship of false gods?
- a) Asa
- b) Manasseh
- c) Kong
- d) Jehoram

A New Temple

373. **FUNTASTIC FACT!** Ezra was a leader, a scribe, and a contemporary of Nehemiah, as well as a teacher, studier, and follower of God's Word. He kept his focus on the Lord, and he accomplished much.

374. True or False: The book of Ezra mentions Ezra in its first verse.

375. The book of Ezra opens with
- a) Christ's birth
- b) the end of the Jews' captivity in Babylon
- c) a psalm of David
- d) a prophecy about the end of the world

376. Who decreed a new temple would be built in Jerusalem?

377. After this decree, how many people returned to the land?

378. True or False: No one opposed rebuilding God's temple.

379. True or False: The new temple would be even greater and more beautiful than the one Solomon built.

380. Artaxerxes was king of
   a) Israel
   b) Persia
   c) Babylon
   d) Cupcakes

381. Was Artaxerxes as friendly to Israel as King Cyrus?

382. Israel's enemies let King Artaxerxes know Jerusalem was being rebuilt by
   a) blowing trumpets until Persia's walls fell down
   b) a comedy routine delivered by a clown
   c) sending a letter
   d) text

383. FUNTASTIC FACT! The name Ezra means "Jehovah helps."

384. King Artaxerxes found the city of Jerusalem to be
   a) peaceful
   b) fun loving
   c) dirty
   d) rebellious

385. Was King Artaxerxes's observation true?

386. King Artaxerxes ordered that
  a) a festival be held each year to honor Jerusalem
  b) everyone in Persia was to worship Jehovah
  c) the city not be rebuilt until his command
  d) no Jew was to work more than eight hours
     a day

387. True or False: The rebuilding was stopped until the second year of the reign of King Darius.

388. When the Jews began rebuilding the temple during Darius's reign, did anyone question their actions?

389. The king said the Israelites were also to be given
  a) thirty minutes off to watch TV each day
  b) whatever they needed to make sacrifices to God
  c) two daily servings each of fruits and vegetables
  d) new shoes

NEHEMIAH BUILDS A WALL

390. FUNTASTIC FACT! The book of Nehemiah was written about 430 BC by Nehemiah.

391. In Nehemiah's time, the Jews in Jerusalem were
  a) rich
  b) happy
  c) suffering
  d) in charge of all of Jerusalem's fast-food
     restaurants

392. True or False: When the book of Nehemiah begins, the walls of Jerusalem have just been built.

393. True or False: Nehemiah asked the Lord to allow the king to have mercy on him.

394. When he heard about the people's plight, Nehemiah
- a) wept and prayed to God
- b) ran away to Tarsus
- c) recommended a doctor
- d) fled and ended up in the belly of a fish

395. Nehemiah was the king's
- a) food taster
- b) cupbearer
- c) jester
- d) deejay

396. King Artaxerxes noticed that Nehemiah
- a) had spilled spaghetti on the palace's white carpet
- b) looked sad
- c) had the ability to interpret dreams
- d) had written him a message on the wall

397. Nehemiah asked the king if he could
- a) give the Israelites straw to help them make better bricks
- b) borrow some money
- c) go back and rebuild the city of Jerusalem
- d) give the Jews more vacation time

398. Did the king grant Nehemiah's request?

399. True or False: Nehemiah told the king he was sad about Jerusalem.

400. FUNTASTIC FACT! Traveling to Judah would have placed Nehemiah in great danger. Nehemiah needed letters from the king giving him permission to pass through enemy territory. The king also sent along soldiers to protect Nehemiah from harm (Nehemiah 2:7-9).

401. The animal Nehemiah took with him was
   a) his pet goldfish
   b) his donkey
   c) a camel with bad breath
   d) a boa constrictor to squeeze his opponents
      to death

402. True or False: Rebuilding Jerusalem was risky because it was against the emperor's wishes.

403. Who was Nehemiah counting on for his success?

404. The wall was built in a circle, starting and finishing at
   a) the community pool
   b) David's tomb
   c) a statue of a unicorn
   d) the sheep gate

405. True or False: Everyone was happy to see the new wall being built.

406. True or False: When Nehemiah realized that people were making fun of his efforts to rebuild the wall, he called off the project and went back to Persia.

407. Later, Jerusalem's Jews complained that
    a) they were too poor to feed their families
    b) they had gotten tired of manna
    c) there was a big line for the restroom
    d) the wall should be painted gold

408. Nehemiah was angry when he discovered
    a) the leaders had been keeping all the gold
       paint for themselves
    b) his favorite restaurant went out of business
    c) the rich Jews were taking advantage of their
       poor relatives
    d) his palace had been destroyed

409. True or False: The leaders promised to return everyone's property and not try to collect any debts.

410. To show how God would punish any leader who didn't keep his promise to help the poor, Nehemiah
    a) shook his fist
    b) shook his sash
    c) invented a new dance move
    d) told the people how to make milkshakes

411. Did the leaders keep their promise to help the poor?

412. True or False: Nehemiah took advantage of all the privileges he was entitled to as governor of Judah.

413. FUNTASTIC FACT! Nehemiah did not claim his big allowance because he knew that the people already had enough burdens without him claiming a large amount of money and land for himself (Nehemiah 5:18). This is in contrast to the way the rich Jews were treating their relatives in Jerusalem.

414. How many days did it take to build the entire wall?

MORE QUEENS OF THE BIBLE

415. How many queens are mentioned in Esther?

416. True or False: Queen Vashti willingly joined the king's feast so he could show her beauty to everyone present.

417. After Esther became queen, Mordecai found favor by
    a) doubling the grapes produced by the king's vineyards
    b) winning a hot dog-eating contest
    c) foiling an assassination attempt on the king
    d) storing enough grain to take the provinces through a seven-year famine

418. FUNTASTIC FACT! Esther's act of speaking to the king was so courageous because simply asking to speak to him could have resulted in her death (Esther 4:11).

419. True or False: Haman was worried about attending Esther's banquets.

420. Why did Queen Vashti lose favor with King Xerxes?
     a) she embarrassed him in front of another king
     b) she ate up all his candy stash
     c) she refused to come when Xerxes sent for her
     d) she sold his favorite horse

421. When Queen Esther came unannounced to see King Xerxes, she would be killed unless the king did what?

422. Fill in the blanks (same word): Esther said, "I will go to the king, though it is against the law, and if I _____, I _____."

423. After Queen Esther identified Haman as her enemy to King Xerxes, what did Haman do that enraged King Xerxes even more?
     a) tried to escape by entering the women's court
     b) appealed to Esther and fell on her couch
     c) asked palace guards to hide him
     d) used the king's ring to forge a document refuting Esther's claim

424. How many queens of Israel are mentioned by name?

425. How many queens of Judah are mentioned by name?

426. How are those two queens related?
   a) sisters
   b) mother and daughter
   c) cousins
   d) aunt and niece

427. What horrible thing did Athaliah do?

428. Which wicked queen practiced witchcraft?

DANIEL

◇◇◇◇◇◇◇◇◇◇

429. FUNTASTIC FACT! Daniel's Babylonian name was Belteshazzar (Daniel 1:7).

430. Fill in the blank: "Daniel _____ that he would not defile himself with the king's food, or with the wine that he drank."

431. How many days did Daniel and his friends eat the food they requested as a test?
   a) three
   b) seven
   c) ten
   d) fourteen

432. True or False: Because Daniel interpreted Nebuchadnezzar's dream, Nebuchadnezzar made Daniel "ruler over the whole province of Babylon and chief prefect over all the wise men of Babylon."

433. Who was the king of Persia when Daniel was thrown into the lions' den?
- a) Darius
- b) Artaxerxes
- c) Shalmaneser
- d) Sennacherib

434. Choose A or B: The people who tried to find fault in Daniel were (a) magicians and sorcerers or (b) government leaders.

435. True or False: The men knew they couldn't find any fault against Daniel unless it had to do with the law of Daniel's God.

436. True or False: The king was tricked into passing a law stating that no one could ask a petition of anyone but him for thirty days.

437. How many times a day did Daniel kneel and pray?
- a) one
- b) two
- c) three
- d) four

438. True or False: The king was eager to have Daniel thrown into the lions' den.

439. Who said to Daniel, "May your God, whom you serve so faithfully, rescue you"?

440. Whom did God send to shut the lions' mouths?

441. True or False: The king had the men who accused Daniel thrown into the lions' den.

442. True or False: Daniel was a prince of Judah before he was taken to Babylon.

FieRY FURNACE

443. The image Nebuchadnezzar erected on the plain of Dura was made of
    a) wood
    b) brass
    c) gold
    d) ivory

444. Fill in the blank: Any time the people heard music, they were to _____ the image.

445. Who told the king that Shadrach, Meshach, and Abednego refused to bow down and worship the image?
    a) magicians
    b) Chaldeans
    c) Jews
    d) princes

446. Who said, "We do not need to defend ourselves before you in this matter. If we are thrown into the blazing furnace, the God we serve is able to deliver us from it, and he will deliver us from Your Majesty's hand"?

447. True or False: Nebuchadnezzar commanded that the furnace be heated three times hotter than normal.

448. Who was commanded to bind Shadrach, Meshach, and Abednego?
   a) servants
   b) mighty men
   c) ogres
   d) slaves

449. True or False: The hot fire killed the people who threw Shadrach, Meshach, and Abednego into the fiery furnace.

450. FUNTASTIC FACT! Nebuchadnezzar made a decree that anyone who spoke against the God of Shadrach, Meshach, and Abednego would be torn "limb from limb" (Daniel 3:29 ESV).

JONAH AND THE WHALE

451. FUNTASTIC FACT! More than 120,000 people lived in Nineveh in Jonah's time (Jonah 4:11).

452. Who told Jonah to go to Nineveh?

453. Jonah was instructed to tell the Ninevites that
   a) they had found grace in the eyes of the Lord
   b) the Lord was against their wickedness
   c) they were to build an ark to prepare for an oncoming flood
   d) they were to build a temple in God's honor

454. Instead of going to Nineveh, Jonah went where?
 a) Joppa
 b) Tarshish
 c) fishing
 d) Susa

455. Jonah boarded a ship to Tarshish because
 a) Tarshish was on the way to Nineveh
 b) he wanted a vacation cruise
 c) he wanted to flee from the Lord
 d) he needed a catch of fish to take along as food

456. What happened to the sea after Jonah boarded the ship?

457. What was Jonah swallowed by?

458. How many days and nights was Jonah in the belly of the great fish?

459. Jonah told the Ninevites that they had how many days left before God would destroy them?

460. After the Ninevites heard the message from God delivered by Jonah, they
 a) threw Jonah out of town
 b) stoned Jonah
 c) fasted and wore sackcloth
 d) proclaimed the Lord was greater than Baal

461. True or False: The king of Nineveh resisted God's call to repentance.

462. Nineveh's repentance angered Jonah because
a) Nineveh wasn't part of his own country
b) his ex-wife lived in Nineveh
c) success meant he would be required to join the priesthood
d) the Ninevites didn't invite him to their revival service

463. True or False: Jonah asked God to take his life.

464. Why did Jonah remain near Nineveh?

465. The plant that shaded Jonah was destroyed by
a) a bolt of lightning
b) a worm
c) flies
d) harsh sunlight

ANGELS OF THE BIBLE

466. FUNTASTIC FACT! One of the main jobs an angel has is to be a spirit sent forth to minister to those who will inherit salvation (Hebrews 1:14).

467. Fill in the blank: "The angel of the LORD encamps around those who _____ him."

468. According to 2 Samuel 14:20, which of the following is an attribute of the angel of the Lord?
a) strength
b) might
c) wisdom
d) love of God

469. How many times did the angel of the Lord speak to Abraham during the attempted sacrifice of Isaac?

470. What animal saw the angel of the Lord?
   a) a dog
   b) a duck
   c) a donkey
   d) a deer

471. Fill in the blank: In Isaiah 63:9, Isaiah calls the angel of the Lord "the angel of His _____."

472. True or False: When the angel of the Lord went before the children of Israel in the wilderness, the angel took the form of a pillar of cloud.

473. How many angels went to save Lot from the destruction of his city?

474. What did the angel of the Lord tell Paul when the ship he was on was in a bad storm?
   a) "You all need your life jackets."
   b) "You will all be saved."
   c) "You will run aground."
   d) "You will not be shipwrecked."

475. To whom did the angel of the Lord appear and then ascend to heaven in the flame from the altar?
   a) Samson's father
   b) Solomon
   c) Moses
   d) Elijah

476. How many types of angels are mentioned in the Bible?
- a) one
- b) one hundred
- c) three
- d) one million

477. What type of angel was on top of the ark of the covenant?

478. In Hebrews 13:2, why are we told to practice hospitality?

479. The angels have charge over the righteous to do what?
- a) keep you in all your ways
- b) bear you up in their hands
- c) take you to heaven
- d) a & b

480. What angel is described in the book of Daniel as "one of the chief princes"?

481. Who can appear as an angel of light?

482. In David's time, God sent an angel to Jerusalem to do what?
- a) anoint Solomon to be the next king
- b) destroy the city
- c) save David from the Philistines
- d) give David a special message

483. What prophet referred to the cherubim as "living creatures"?

484. How many wings do cherubim have?

485. How many wings do seraphim have?

486. What did the angels do when God created the world?
  a) wept
  b) threw a party
  c) left
  d) shouted for joy

487. In Revelation 5:11 and 7:11, where were the angels in heaven standing?

488. How many angels appeared to the women who came to Jesus' tomb?

489. Why did an angel appear to Zechariah the prophet?
  a) to answer his question
  b) to interpret Zechariah's visions
  c) to show Zechariah visions
  d) all of the above

490. How many angels told the disciples that Jesus would return in the same manner as He left?

491. How many angels appeared to the shepherds to announce Jesus' birth?

492. True or False: Jesus said children have angels who see the Father's face in heaven.

493. What do the angels in heaven do?

494. What does Psalm 78:24–25 refer to as angels' food?
    a) angel food cake, of course!
    b) ice cream
    c) manna
    d) fish

495. What devout Gentile saw an angel?

496. FUNTASTIC FACT! Angels long to look into the ways of God (1 Peter 1:12)!

497. Who will judge the angels?

498. In Revelation 10:6, an angel declared that
    a) the kingdom of God had come
    b) Jesus is King of Kings
    c) there will be no more delay
    d) all of the above

FAMINES

499. FUNTASTIC FACT! A famine is an extreme shortage of food.

500. Where did Abram go to escape a famine in his land?
    a) a buffet
    b) Canada
    c) Egypt
    d) the North Pole

501. Where did Isaac go to escape famine?
    a) McDonald's
    b) Japan
    c) Egypt
    d) the land of the Philistines

502. Who managed the store of provisions in Egypt during the seven-year famine?

503. True or False: Famine struck Gilgal during the days of Elijah.

504. To what land did Naomi and her husband go to escape famine in Judah?
    a) Disneyland
    b) Finland
    c) an island
    d) Moab

505. Fill in the blank: During David's reign, a famine occurred that lasted _____ years?

506. True or False: A famine occurred in the early days of the church.

AMAZING ANIMALS

◇◇◇◇◇◇◇◇◇◇◇◇◇◇◇◇◇◇◇◇◇◇◇◇◇◇◇◇◇◇◇◇

507. FUNTASTIC FACT! The King James Version of the Bible mentions a unicorn (Psalm 92:10)!

508. What kind of animals helped Samson burn the grain fields of his enemies?

509. What animal were the Israelites not to muzzle as it was treading grain?

510. What did Peter see inside a sheet, coming down from heaven by its four corners?

511. Fill in the blank: After Adam and Eve sinned, God provided clothing for them made of _____.

512. What animal did God provide as a substitute burnt offering as Abraham prepared to offer Isaac?

513. What animal spoke to Balaam when it saw the angel of the Lord?

514. Fill in the blank: The psalmist said he longed for God even as a _____ panted for water brooks.

515. What animal did Jesus ride for His triumphal entry into Jerusalem?

516. What is the strongest of beasts, according to Proverbs?

517. What animal did Goliath compare himself to when he saw David approaching him?

518. What creature of the wilderness does Malachi describe as laying waste to Esau's heritage?

519. What colors are the four horses mentioned in Revelation 6?

520. What animals did Jesus ask His disciples to ask a man for?

521. Fill in the blank: Jesus said it was easier for a _____ to go through the eye of a needle than for a rich man to enter heaven.

SHEEP
◇◇◇◇◇◇◇◇◇

522. Isaiah said that "All we like sheep have" what?

523. True or False: The story of the lost sheep can be found in Matthew and Luke.

524. Fill in the blank: "What man of you, having a hundred sheep, if he has lost one of them, does not leave the ninety-nine in the open country, and go after the one that is lost, until he _____ it?"

525. Fill in the blank: When he worked for Laban, Jacob agreed to take all the _____ sheep as his pay.

526. When the sheep is found, the shepherd rejoices and lays it
    a) in the manger
    b) upon the hay
    c) by its mother
    d) on his shoulders

527. Who said, "I am the good shepherd. The good shepherd lays down his life for the sheep"?

528. How did Jesus describe one who enters the sheepfold other than by the door?

529. Fill in the blank: "But he who enters by the door is the _____."

530. Fill in the blank: Jesus said, "My sheep hear my voice, and I know them, and they _____."

531. Fill in the blank: For one judgment, Jesus said that all the nations will be gathered before Him, and the people will be separated like sheep are separated from _____.

532. Fill in the blank: Peter said we were like sheep gone astray but now we are returned to the Shepherd and Overseer of our _____.

SHEPHERDS

533. Fill in the blank: "The LORD is my _____; I shall not want."

534. Why did the psalmist say he would "fear no evil" in spite of walking in the "valley of the shadow of death"?

535. Who wrote, "When the chief Shepherd appears, you will receive the unfading crown of glory"?

536. How did the Egyptians feel about shepherds?
  a) they were BFFs
  b) they tolerated them
  c) they thought they were an abomination
  d) there were no shepherds in Egypt

537. Fill in the blanks: Jesus is called the _____ Shepherd, the _____ Shepherd, and the _____ Shepherd.

538. Fill in the blank: "He will gather the _____ in his arms."

539. How did Zechariah describe the worthless shepherd?

540. To whom was Jesus speaking when He said, "I will strike the Shepherd, and the sheep of the flock will be scattered"?

TReeS

541. On what day of creation did God create flowers and plants?

542. What flower did Jesus say was better arrayed than Solomon in all his glory?

543. Peter says, "The grass withers, and its flower falls away," but what endures forever?

544. What plants did Moses' mother hide him among?

545. What tree is mentioned in Genesis and Revelation?

546. What three trees are specifically mentioned in the garden of Eden?

547. What kind of tree did Deborah sit under?

548. True or False: The Bible mentions apple trees.

549. Isaiah 55:12 says that all the trees of the field will what?

550. What kind of tree did Zacchaeus climb so he could see Jesus?

seas

xxxxxx

551. Psalm 104:25 says the great and wide sea is full of
   a) innumerable things
   b) teeming things
   c) living things great and small
   d) all of the above

552. Those who go down to the sea in ships see what?
   a) the works of the Lord
   b) other ships
   c) God's wonders in the deep
   d) a & c

553. True or False: God assigned the sea a limit.

554. What group of people drowned in the Red Sea?

555. What will fill the earth as waters cover the sea?

556. Fill in the blanks: In John's vision of heaven, he saw a sea of _____ like _____ before the throne of God.

557. True or False: When the first heaven and earth pass away, there will be no more sea.

558. Which of the following were also names for the sea of Galilee?
   a) the Great Sea
   b) Chinnereth
   c) Gennesaret
   d) b & c

559. What we refer to today as the Dead Sea is called what in the Bible?

DREAMS
◇◇◇◇◇◇◇◇◇◇◇◇

560. Jacob dreamed of a _____ that went to heaven.
   a) staircase
   b) ladder
   c) mountain
   d) chariot

561. Pharaoh dreamed that seven skinny _____ ate seven fat _____.
   a) cattle
   b) sheep
   c) horses
   d) fish

562. Who had a dream about seven heads of plump grain and seven heads of thin grain?

563. Who saw a sheet full of creatures and was told to "rise and eat"?
   a) John
   b) Peter
   c) Stephen
   d) James

564. Who was warned in a dream not to go back to Herod?
    a) wise men
    b) shepherds
    c) Joseph
    d) John the Baptist

565. Who was told in a dream to take a wife, even though she was expecting a child?
    a) Hosea
    b) Joseph
    c) Moses
    d) Jacob

566. Who was disturbed because she had a dream about Jesus?
    a) Mary Magdalene
    b) Martha
    c) Herodias
    d) Pilate's wife

567. In Daniel's prophetic dream of kingdoms to come, how many beasts did Daniel see?
    a) two
    b) three
    c) four
    d) seven

568. True or False: Joseph's first dream was that animals bowed down to him.

569. What was Jacob's reaction to Joseph's dream of the sun, moon, and eleven stars bowing to him?

570. How many dreams of his own did Joseph have?

571. Where were Joseph, the butler, and the baker when Joseph interpreted their dreams for them?

572. In the Midianite's dream that Gideon overheard, what happened to the Midianite's tent?
    a) a burning lantern consumed it
    b) a flood from the Jordan River washed it away
    c) a round loaf of barley bread overturned it
    d) a statue with feet of clay fell on it

573. Whose wife said she had suffered many things in a dream because of Jesus?
    a) the wife of Caiaphas
    b) the wife of Herod
    c) the wife of Pilate
    d) the wife of George Washington

574. When Nebuchadnezzar had his dream, whom did he call to tell him what it was?
    a) magicians
    b) astrologers
    c) sorcerers
    d) all of the above

575. Why were Nebuchadnezzar's astrologers unable to give an interpretation of his dream?
    a) Daniel told them to remain silent
    b) Nebuchadnezzar would not tell them the contents of the dream
    c) they feared telling Nebuchadnezzar that his kingdom would crumble
    d) Nebuchadnezzar's rivals threatened them

GOOD COURAGE

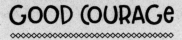

576. Who told the Israelites to be of good courage?

577. Who told Joshua to be of good courage?

578. True or False: Upon becoming their leader, Joshua told the Israelites that he had courage.

579. True or False: Joshua told his army that if they had courage, the Lord would fight for them.

580. Upon what occasion did David tell Solomon to be of good courage?

581. When Hezekiah told his army to be of good courage, what nation was coming after them?
   a) Assyria
   b) Babylon
   c) Egypt
   d) Persia

582. Which church did Paul, in his letter to that church, tell to be brave and strong?

FEAR NOT!

Match the person to the occasion when someone told them not to fear:

583. Hagar
584. Joseph's brothers
585. Joshua
586. Gideon
587. Solomon
588. Paul

a) commanded to build the temple
b) afraid of being attacked
c) needed water
d) feared revenge
e) became the leader
f) fear of death

MIRACLES

589. Jesus' first recorded miracle was at Cana of Galilee. What was it?

590. Who asked Jesus to perform His first miracle?
a) Joseph
b) Mary
c) Elijah
d) a nervous bridegroom

591. How many fish were caught in the net in the miracle of the filling of the fishing nets?

592. Before Jesus calmed the sea, what was He doing?

593. What did Jesus say to calm the sea?

594. True or False: The five thousand were fed with five loaves and two fish.

595. Who found the boy with the loaves and fish?
    a) a shepherd
    b) Andrew
    c) Jesus
    d) Simon Peter

596. How many baskets of food were left over after the feeding of the five thousand?

597. After Jesus sent the multitude away and the disciples crossed by ship to the other side of the sea without Jesus, what did they see in the fourth watch of the night?

598. Because of what miracle did the Sanhedrin plot to take Jesus' life?

599. What two people had time altered for them?

600. What two Old Testament men didn't die?

601. What miracle was performed by both Peter and Paul?
    a) making a city vanish
    b) casting out demons
    c) curing a lame man
    d) b & c

602. What Old Testament prophet fed one hundred men with twenty loaves of bread and had some left over?

603. Who cured bad water with salt?

604. On what mountain was Moses when he saw the burning bush?
    a) Carmel
    b) Horeb
    c) Everest
    d) Moriah

605. Filled with compassion, Jesus performed what miracle during the funeral procession for the widow's son?

606. What miracle did Peter perform in Joppa that spread Jesus' name in that city?

607. What miracle occurred in the heavens the day Joshua and the Israelites defeated the armies of the Amorites?
    a) stars collided
    b) the moon fell down
    c) the sun stood still
    d) all the birds started dancing

608. While Jesus had given the disciples authority to perform miracles in His name, what did He want them to rejoice about instead?

609. Which of Moses' miracles were Pharaoh's magicians *not* able to imitate?
   a) bringing forth gnats to cover men and beasts
   b) changing their staffs into snakes
   c) turning water into blood
   d) making frogs come up over the land

610. The supernatural miracle God performed to help Joshua and his men successfully defend the Gibeonites was what?
   a) made the sun stand still and stopped the moon
   b) struck the enemy soldiers with a plague
   c) divided the waters of the Jordan
   d) infested the land with gibbons

LET THERE BE LIGHT

611. Who fought a battle with torches hidden in pitchers?

612. Fill in the blank: John said if we walk in the light as Jesus is in the light, then we have _____ with one another.

613. Who said, "You are the light of the world"?

614. Why are we to let our light shine before men?

615. Fill in the blanks: Jesus said people do not light a lamp and put it under a _____ but on a _____.

616. What do the seven lampstands in Revelation 1:20 represent?

617. Fill in the blanks: Paul said that when the Lord comes, He will bring to light the _____ things of _____.

TALKING TO GOD

618. True or False: We can pray to God anytime.

619. When we pray to God, we should first
   a) praise Him
   b) ask for whatever we want
   c) ask for bad weather so school will close
   d) tell Him we haven't done anything wrong

620. What Old Testament book contains many songs and prayers?

621. Most of the psalms were written by
   a) David
   b) Adam
   c) Moses
   d) Mary

622. FUNTASTIC FACT! When you worship and pray with other people in your congregation, it is called *corporate worship*. Although praying alone is important, corporate worship is one way to take part in the Christian community.

623. True or False: In Old Testament times, people never prayed directly to God.

624. True or False: Abraham's servant asked for God's guidance when he was told to choose a wife for Isaac.

625. After Isaac married Rebekah, Isaac prayed for
    a) a gym membership
    b) a puppy
    c) permission to join the Canaanite Bowling League
    d) Rebekah to have a baby

626. When we go to God in prayer, we should
    a) be humble
    b) convince Him how great we are
    c) give Him a list of our accomplishments in church
    d) tell Him all about the latest *Star Wars* movie

627. FUNTASTIC FACT! When we ask God for something, it is called a *petition*. Although God wants us to express our wants and needs to Him, our prayers should not be full of petitions without praise or thanksgiving. Not every prayer needs to have a petition. You can simply give thanks to God or praise Him.

628. True or False: When Jonah was in trouble, he prayed to God.

629. True or False: Before Jesus was crucified, He prayed that God would change His mind about allowing Him to die in such a horrible way.

630. True or False: The Bible tells us that Jesus had an active prayer life.

631. Jesus often prayed
    a) loudly, so all would hear
    b) alone
    c) only with His disciples, or else others would learn how to pray
    d) only in church

632. The Bible tells of a Pharisee who prayed
    a) loudly, boasting about his goodness
    b) silently
    c) in French, a language unheard of at that time
    d) for God to have mercy upon him

633. Regarding enemies, Jesus said we are to
    a) love them
    b) bless them
    c) pray for them
    d) all of the above

634. True or False: When you pray, you should always give thanks to God.

635. Name five things you can thank God for today.

QUESTIONS GOD ASKED

To whom was God speaking when He asked the following questions:

636. Where were you when I laid the foundations of the earth?

637. Where are you?

638. Why are you so angry?

639. What is that in your hand?

640. Ask! What shall I give you?

641. From where do you come?

642. Is it right for you to be angry?

643. How have I wearied you?

644. Whom shall I send? Who will go for us?

645. Is anything too hard for the Lord?

CHILDREN

646. FUNTASTIC FACT! Jesus loves children! He said, "Let the little children come to me, and do not hinder them, for the kingdom of heaven belongs to such as these" (Matthew 19:14 NIV).

647. How old was the youngest king of Judah when he began to reign?
   a) seven
   b) eight
   c) ten
   d) twelve

648. How old was the second youngest king of Judah when he began to reign?
   a) eight
   b) ten
   c) twelve
   d) fourteen

649. How old was Jairus's daughter when Jesus raised her from the dead?

650. Psalm 127:3 says that children are a _____ from the Lord.
   a) gift
   b) blessing
   c) heritage
   d) curse

651. Who said, "For this child I prayed"?
   a) Hannah
   b) Sarah
   c) Elizabeth
   d) Mary

652. In what way should a child be raised up?

653. What child, when he was called in the night, said, "Speak, for Your servant hears"?

654. What did these children have in common: Ishmael, Isaac, Samson, John the Baptist, Jesus?

655. In Isaiah 11:6 (KJV), it says, "A little child shall lead them." What will the child lead?
   a) animals
   b) adults
   c) children
   d) a parade

THE BIRTH OF JESUS

656. True or False: The story of Jesus' birth is found in the book of Matthew.

657. FUNTASTIC FACT! There were fourteen generations from Abraham to David, fourteen from David to the exile in Babylon, and fourteen from then to Jesus' birth (Matthew 1:17).

658. When she discovered she would give birth to Jesus, Mary was engaged to
    a) Adam
    b) Joseph
    c) Moses
    d) Lot

659. Who first told Mary she would have a baby?

660. True or False: Mary visited her cousin Elizabeth in Judea after she discovered she would give birth to God's son.

661. True or False: In a dream, an angel told Joseph he should not be afraid to take Mary as his wife.

662. FUNTASTIC FACT! Jesus was born in the same town as King David (Luke 2:4).

663. In which town was Jesus born?

664. Joseph and Mary went to Bethlehem before Jesus was born because
    a) they were on vacation
    b) a census was being taken
    c) they won a new car in a contest
    d) Joseph had been offered a job as an innkeeper

665. True or False: King Herod was filled with joy when he was told the news of Jesus' birth.

666. Fill in the blanks: The wise men brought Jesus gifts of _____, _____, and _____.

667. True or False: When Mary and Joseph arrived in town, they stayed at the best hotel.

668. The shepherds learned about Jesus' birth from
    a) a talking wolf
    b) an invitation to His baby shower
    c) angels
    d) Mary

669. **FUNTASTIC FACT!** Luke traced Jesus' ancestors all the way back to Adam! You can find the record of Jesus' lineage in Luke 3:23–38.

670. True or False: The wise men told King Herod where Jesus was.

671. True or False: Mary selected Jesus' name herself.

672. After Jesus was born, an angel told Joseph in a dream to take his family to
    a) Egypt
    b) Sodom
    c) China
    d) the North Pole

673. Joseph, Mary, and Jesus stayed in Egypt until Herod
    a) bought them all new ponies
    b) said he was sorry
    c) promised not to kill Jesus
    d) died

674. FUNTASTIC FACT! Joseph was first told in a dream to go to Israel after Herod's death. In a second dream, he was told to go to Galilee. The family settled there in the town of Nazareth (Matthew 2:22-23).

675. Fill in the blank: Jesus was called a _____ because He grew up in Nazareth.

676. True or False: When Joseph and Mary presented the baby Jesus to the Lord, they sacrificed a pair of doves and two young pigeons.

677. Mary and Joseph offered the sacrifice because
    a) it showed their love for each other
    b) they could not find a young ram to sacrifice
    c) it was required by Mosaic law
    d) they had no silver for the treasury

678. What godly man was told he would not die before he saw the Messiah?

679. Jesus was presented to the Lord at the temple in
    a) Nazareth
    b) Jerusalem
    c) Bethlehem
    d) Egypt

680. True or False: When the baby Jesus was presented at the temple, two people said that Jesus was the Messiah.

Jesus GROWS UP

681. FUNTASTIC FACT! Luke is the only Gospel writer who tells us about Jesus' childhood. You can find the story in Luke 2:39–52.

682. True or False: The books of the Bible that tell us about Jesus' life and ministry are called the Gospels.

683. Jesus grew up in the town of
    a) Bethlehem
    b) Cairo
    c) Paris
    d) Nazareth

684. Jesus' parents went to Jerusalem every year to celebrate the
    a) birth of Jesus
    b) Last Supper
    c) Passover
    d) Super Bowl

685. After their trip to Jerusalem when Jesus was twelve, his parents discovered He was not with their group returning to their home in Nazareth. They went back to Jerusalem to look for Him. How long did it take them to find Him?

686. Joseph and Mary found Jesus
    a) in the temple, amazing the teachers with His wisdom
    b) at the home of a relative
    c) in a small house with a sign that read LOST AND FOUND
    d) eating doughnuts at a police station

687. True or False: Jesus was surprised that Mary and Joseph did not know He would be in the temple.

688. One man who was important in Jesus' earthly life was
  a) John the Baptist
  b) John the Methodist
  c) John the Presbyterian
  d) John the Lutheran

689. FUNTASTIC FACT! When John the Baptist was born, his father planned to name him Zechariah. The Holy Spirit led his parents to name him John instead (Luke 1:59–63).

690. John the Baptist ate
  a) granola bars and yogurt
  b) beef and cheese
  c) fried bees and ants
  d) locusts and wild honey

691. True or False: John the Baptist preached about Jesus.

692. True or False: John the Baptist said Jesus would baptize with the Holy Spirit.

693. When John the Baptist preached about King Herod, he said that Herod
  a) was a fine king, worthy of worship
  b) had kept his promise to give every student an iPad
  c) was evil
  d) had paid John to say good things about him

694. What happened to John the Baptist after he preached about King Herod?

695. Who baptized Jesus?

696. After Jesus was baptized, the Holy Spirit came upon Him in the form of
    a) a raven
    b) an angel
    c) glitter
    d) a dove

697. True or False: Jesus turned stones into bread to show the devil He was God's Son.

698. Satan tempted Jesus by asking Him to turn stones into bread because
    a) Satan's bread had burned in the flames of hell
    b) Jesus' bread would be far better than any bread Satan could make
    c) Jesus was very hungry and wanted to eat because He had not eaten for forty days
    d) Satan's bread tasted like cardboard

699. True or False: When Satan told Jesus to jump from the top of the temple, Jesus told him that we are not to test God.

700. If Jesus would worship Satan, Satan promised to give Jesus
    a) all the world's kingdoms
    b) bags of gold
    c) heaven's gates
    d) no homework forever

701. Who helped Jesus after He was tempted by Satan?

702. FUNTASTIC FACT! Jesus was about thirty years old when He began His ministry (Luke 3:23).

703. Where did Jesus begin His ministry?

JESUS TELLS US ABOUT ENEMIES

704. True or False: Jesus says we should not take revenge on our enemies but ask God to get back at them instead.

705. Jesus says we should lend money to
  a) our enemies, without expecting anything in return
  b) our enemies, but only once
  c) only our friends, since our enemies are mean
  d) no one

706. True or False: Our reward for being kind to enemies will be a slap in the face.

707. Jesus says that God
  a) shows mercy only to those who love Him
  b) remembers only those who thank Him for His goodness
  c) is kind to everyone, including the evil and unthankful
  d) will destroy our enemies if we ask Him

708. True or False: Jesus teaches that when people say mean things to you or about you, you should be kind to them anyway.

709. A publican is a
    a) tax collector
    b) celebrity
    c) clerk at the public library
    d) teacher at the public school

710. FUNTASTIC FACT! One of Jesus' twelve disciples was a publican. "As he walked along, he saw Levi son of Alphaeus sitting at the tax collector's booth. 'Follow me,' Jesus told him, and Levi got up and followed him" (Mark 2:14 NIV). As you can see from the verse, Matthew was also known as Levi.

711. True or False: Since it was important that Jesus not damage His reputation as God's Son, He avoided associating with outcasts and sinners while here on earth.

712. Jesus teaches that we should
    a) not do anything extra for our enemies but the bare minimum
    b) love our friends more than our enemies
    c) give our enemies New Testament Bibles
    d) go the extra mile for our enemies and show them much love

713. True or False: We don't have to forgive anybody who doesn't ask us for forgiveness.

714. When Jesus speaks of neighbors, He means
   a) the people who live in the house next to yours
   b) everyone
   c) the people who live in your town
   d) your enemies

715. Jesus teaches that the first great commandment is
   a) don't get mad, get even
   b) never forget the bad things someone has done to you
   c) love God with all your heart, soul, and mind
   d) don't let the sun go down on your anger

716. According to Jesus, people will know we are His disciples when we
   a) get three perfect attendance pins at church
   b) love one another
   c) go to vacation Bible school every year
   d) listen to Christian radio stations every day

717. Which of Jesus' disciples betrayed Him? (To _betray_ means to deliver someone to an enemy.)

718. When Jesus' disciple betrayed Him, the disciple received
   a) an all-expenses paid vacation
   b) a houseful of new furniture
   c) thirty pieces of silver
   d) a chance to appear on a TV game show

719. According to Matthew's Gospel, when Jesus was betrayed He said,
   a) "Friend, do what you came to do."
   b) "I am innocent!"
   c) "Why did you kiss me on the cheek? Gross!"
   d) "This means I'm down to eleven disciples."

PARABLES

◇◇◇◇◇◇◇◇◇◇◇◇◇◇

720. FUNTASTIC FACT! A parable is a story that teaches a lesson.

721. Jesus taught in parables so
  a) those who didn't love God wouldn't understand His teachings
  b) He could put them together later in a book
  c) His disciples could sell the rights to them after His resurrection
  d) He would be famous

722. True or False: The disciples always understood the parables without Jesus having to explain them.

723. What parable illustrates how God feels about those who don't forgive others?

724. Under what two places did Jesus say that a lamp should not be put?

725. How many soils are described in the parable of the sower?

726. What three hazards happened to the seeds in Jesus' parable of the sower?

727. In Luke 16, Jesus told a parable of a rich man and of a beggar named what?
  a) Stephanas
  b) Lazarus
  c) Caiaphas
  d) Cornelius

728. In Jesus' illustration of how God wants to give us good things, what did the Lord say a father would *not* give his son if he asked for bread?

729. To what did Jesus compare the mustard seed?

THE PRODIGAL SON

◇◇◇◇◇◇◇◇◇◇◇◇◇◇◇◇◇◇◇◇◇◇◇◇◇◇

730. Who told the story of the prodigal son?

731. True or False: Like many of Jesus' stories, the parable of the prodigal son appears more than once in the Bible.

732. **FUNTASTIC FACT!** The word *prodigal* means "recklessly extravagant; lavish."

733. In the story, how many sons did the wealthy man have?

734. The younger son asked his father to
   a) give him his share of his inheritance
   b) let him marry the richest girl in town
   c) allow him to go to the skating rink with the church youth group
   d) loan him some money to go to the mall

735. An inheritance is
   a) a hair transplant
   b) property that is passed on when someone dies
   c) nose hair
   d) Hebrew for "cash"

736. True or False: The father did as the younger son asked.

737. The younger son
    a) invested the money in comic books
    b) bought a cruise ship
    c) wasted his money
    d) buried the money in the backyard

738. After the son's money was gone, he got a job
    a) at a fast-food restaurant
    b) herding sheep
    c) as a used car salesman
    d) tending pigs

739. True or False: When the father saw the son returning, he was angry and told him to leave.

740. When the son returned, the father gave him
    a) a whipping
    b) a pony
    c) a job
    d) a ring, a robe, and shoes

741. True or False: The father threw a big party to celebrate.

742. True or False: The father was so happy to have the younger son home, he forgot all about the older son.

743. When the older son heard about the welcome-home party, he
    a) hired a band to play at the party
    b) hugged and kissed his brother
    c) gave his brother the keys to his car
    d) was angry

744. Why did the older son feel this way?

745. The father said to the older son,
   a) "Leave my house."
   b) "I always liked your younger brother better than you."
   c) "Everything I have is yours and we are close."
   d) "You always were a tattletale."

746. True or False: The father tried to convince the older son to celebrate his brother's homecoming.

THE GOOD SAMARITAN

747. Where can you find the story of the good Samaritan?

748. FUNTASTIC FACT! The road to Jericho was very dangerous. Thieves and bandits could hide in its mountainous terrain, waiting to rob travelers. This is probably why it is the setting for the parable of the good Samaritan.

749. Jesus told the story of the good Samaritan to answer the question
   a) "Can I follow you?"
   b) "How can I be wise?"
   c) "Is it okay for me to swim right after I eat?"
   d) "Who is my neighbor?"

750. Jesus was asked this question by
   a) a lawyer
   b) a young girl
   c) a blacksmith
   d) a tax collector

751. In the story, a man needed help because he
   a) had eaten too much and had a stomachache
   b) didn't know who his neighbor was
   c) had been beaten and robbed
   d) refused to ask for directions even though he
      was lost

752. True or False: When the priest and the
Levite saw the man lying on the side of the road,
they stopped and helped him.

**753. To what city was the man going when he was
beaten and robbed?** (Hint: The Jews had taken it by
knocking down its walls with the sound of trumpets
and a shout.)

754. Who stopped to help the injured man?

755. FUNTASTIC FACT! The Samaritan was an unlikely
person to help a Jew. Jews were their hated enemies.
This is demonstrated by the Samaritan village that
refused to offer Jesus a place to stay when they discovered He was on His way to Jerusalem. Read Luke
9:51–56 to learn more.

756. True or False: The Samaritan stayed with the
man until the following day.

757. The Samaritan took the man to
   a) dinner at Burger King
   b) a dark alley and robbed him
   c) an inn
   d) a meeting at church

758. How much did the Samaritan give the inn-keeper to care for the man until he was well?

759. FUNTASTIC FACT! Two denarii was equal to two days' pay.

760. True or False: Jesus asked the lawyer to identify which person was the man's neighbor.

761. Who do you think was the neighbor to the man: the priest, the Levite, or the Samaritan?

762. Jesus told the lawyer,
   a) "You look tired."
   b) "Only good people are your neighbors."
   c) "You need to be concerned only about people who are nice to you."
   d) "Go and do likewise."

JESUS HEALS THE SICK

763. FUNTASTIC FACT! The first story about Jesus healing someone is in Matthew 8:1–4.

764. The Bible tells us about Jesus healing sick people in
    a) the Gospels
    b) the Old Testament
    c) Revelation
    d) lots of detail

765. True or False: After He healed the sick man, Jesus commanded him to tell everyone that Jesus was the Messiah.

766. Jesus healed the Roman officer's servant by
    a) touching his cloak
    b) giving him a special medicine
    c) waving a magic wand
    d) giving an order for him to be healed

767. FUNTASTIC FACT! Jesus praised the Roman officer for having great faith (Matthew 8:10).

768. Whose mother-in-law did Jesus heal of a fever?

769. Jesus healed the woman's fever by
    a) touching her forehead
    b) touching her hand
    c) brushing her hair
    d) telling her to bury a potato under a maple tree at midnight

770. FUNTASTIC FACT! After Jesus cured the woman's fever, He healed many others to fulfill a prophecy of Isaiah (Matthew 8:16–17).

771. True or False: When Jesus drove demons from people, the demons proclaimed that Jesus was God's Son.

772. Jesus drove a mob of demons into a
a) herd of pigs
b) school of fish
c) horde of evil people
d) beehive

773. When the local people found out that Jesus had driven the mob of demons out of a man, they
a) feasted for a week
b) were afraid
c) composed a song in His honor
d) made Jesus the town's mayor

774. True or False: After Jesus drove out the demons, the people asked Him to leave their territory.

775. What did the demon-possessed man want to do after Jesus healed him?

776. True or False: Jesus told the man to go back to his family and to tell everyone what God had done for him.

777. Did the man obey Jesus?

778. To get well from an illness she had suffered from for twelve years, a woman touched Jesus'
a) clothing
b) cup
c) feet
d) hand

779. Jesus said the woman had been cured by her
a) money
b) beauty
c) courage
d) faith

780. True or False: When Jesus arrived at the official's house, the little girl had already died.

781. Fill in the blank: Jesus said that the child was not dead but only _____.

782. Right after Jesus brought the little girl back to life, He healed
a) a little boy who had only two fish and a loaf of bread for lunch
b) two blind men
c) three blind mice
d) ten lepers

783. What did Jesus tell the people He healed?

784. Did the people obey Jesus?

THE LORD'S PRAYER

785. FUNTASTIC FACT! You can find the Lord's Prayer in two places in the Bible. You can read it in Matthew 6:9–13 and Luke 11:2–4.

786. Can you recite the Lord's Prayer by heart?

787. Jesus taught the disciples this prayer because
- a) one of them had asked Him to teach them how to pray
- b) He was angered by their awkward prayers
- c) otherwise, they would sing psalms off-key
- d) He was tired of their old ones

788. According to the Lord's Prayer, where is God the Father?

789. What does Jesus mean when He says God's name should be *hallowed*?

790. What do you do to honor God's name?

791. True or False: Obeying God's commandment not to take His name in vain is one way to keep God's name hallowed.

792. True or False: In Matthew's Gospel, Jesus told the crowds how to pray because He was angered by the hypocrites' loud praying.

793. What is a hypocrite?

794. True or False: Once you learn the Lord's Prayer, there is no need to pray on your own.

795. Why is this prayer called "the Lord's Prayer"?

796. When Jesus says we should ask God to forgive us our debts as we forgive our debtors, it means
   a) God should forgive us whether we forgive others or not
   b) we should not owe anyone any money
   c) we should not loan anyone any money
   d) God will forgive us when we forgive others

797. True or False: You are supposed to pray the Lord's Prayer every day on the radio to show how wonderful you are.

THE BEATITUDES

798. FUNTASTIC FACT! The word *beatitude* is defined as a state of bliss. The Beatitudes, which Jesus preached in the Sermon on the Mount, share how to be blessed with utmost bliss.

Fill in the blanks:

799. "Blessed are the _____ ___ _____, for theirs is the kingdom of heaven."

800. "Blessed are those who _____, for they shall be comforted."

801. "Blessed are the _____, for they shall inherit the earth."

802. "Blessed are those who hunger and thirst for _____, for they shall be satisfied."

803. "Blessed are the _____, for they shall receive mercy."

804. "Blessed are the _____ ___ _____, for they shall see God."

805. "Blessed are the _____, for they shall be called sons of God."

806. "Blessed are those who are _____ for righteousness' sake, for theirs is the kingdom of heaven."

807. "Blessed are you when others revile you and persecute you and utter all kinds of _____ against you falsely on my account."

808. "Rejoice and be glad, for your _____ is great in heaven, for so they persecuted the prophets who were before you."

LUKE TELLS US ABOUT JESUS

809. **FUNTASTIC FACT!** Luke also wrote the Acts of the Apostles.

810. **True or False:** Luke is the only Gospel writer to tell us anything about Jesus' boyhood.

811. **True or False:** Jesus healed many people during His ministry on earth.

812. Some important people were mad at Jesus because He ate with
    a) tax collectors and outcasts
    b) no one—He ate alone
    c) His family instead of them
    d) His favorite disciples

813. True or False: Jesus showed us it is all right to prepare food on the Sabbath.

814. To show it is all right to take care of sick people on the Sabbath, Jesus healed
    a) a man with a soccer injury
    b) kids with chicken pox
    c) a man with a paralyzed hand
    d) a computer with a virus

815. True or False: When His enemies saw Jesus healing on the Sabbath, they were happy.

816. A disciple is
    a) a follower
    b) a teacher of false doctrine
    c) an old man
    d) busy

817. Jesus chose twelve disciples. How many of them can you name?

818. Which famous sermon did Jesus preach soon after He chose His disciples?

819. True or False: Jesus said we should hate our enemies.

820. The Bible quotes Jesus as saying, "Do to others as you would have them do to you" (Luke 6:31 NIV). This is called the Golden Rule. What is the meaning of the Golden Rule?

821. True or False: When you see someone who is wrong, you should tell that person right away without worrying about your own faults.

822. While Jesus was visiting Simon the Pharisee, a sinful woman
    a) washed His feet with her tears
    b) tempted Him
    c) yelled at Him
    d) made Him a pie

823. When Simon the Pharisee saw the woman, he
    a) clapped for her
    b) invited her to eat with them
    c) asked her to marry him
    d) thought that Jesus shouldn't let a sinful woman touch Him

824. True or False: Although the woman was sinful, she was trying to show Jesus how much she loved Him.

825. What did Jesus say to the woman after her visit?

826. True or False: Jesus had no followers who were women.

LUKE TELLS US WHAT JESUS SAID

827. True or False: Jesus loved and praised His mother, Mary, over everyone else.

828. When Jesus performed miracles, some people thought He was the resurrected
    a) John the Baptist
    b) Moses
    c) Paul
    d) Lot

829. What does *resurrected* mean?

830. True or False: Jesus predicted His own death and resurrection.

831. FUNTASTIC FACT! When Jesus was praying, His face glowed and His clothes became dazzling white. This is called the transfiguration (Luke 9:29).

832. During the transfiguration, Jesus was visited by
    a) Noah
    b) the three wise men
    c) John the Baptist
    d) Moses and Elijah

833. What did Jesus' visitors talk to Him about?

834. FUNTASTIC FACT! After Jesus was visited during the transfiguration, God's voice came from a cloud. God said, "This is my Son, whom I have chosen; listen to him" (Luke 9:35 NIV).

835. The disciples who saw the transfiguration and heard God's voice
   a) rejoiced and told everyone right away
   b) were afraid and told no one
   c) texted their friends
   d) posted photos on social media

836. True or False: Jesus' disciples wondered who would be the most important among themselves in heaven.

837. Who did Jesus say would be the most important disciple in heaven?

838. When a person who was not a disciple cast out demons in Jesus' name, the disciples
   a) told him to stop
   b) cheered
   c) told him to be wary of demons
   d) tied him to a tree

839. **FUNTASTIC FACT!** It was God's plan for Jesus' death on the cross to take place in Jerusalem. Moses and Elijah talked to Him about it during the transfiguration (Luke 9:30-31). Jesus set out for Jerusalem with God's plan in mind (Luke 9:51).

840. True or False: When a village in Samaria refused to receive Jesus, the disciples pleaded with Jesus to forgive the people of the village.

841. Concerning this village, Jesus told the disciples
 a) to set it on fire
 b) to rename it Petra after Peter
 c) not to be unforgiving toward the citizens
   of the town
 d) that He would eat the Last Supper in this town

842. True or False: After Jesus spoke to the people in the village, they decided to let Him pass through.

843. FUNTASTIC FACT! Jesus chose another seventy-two men to go before Him, two by two, into each town He would be visiting (Luke 10:1).

844. When visiting the towns, Jesus told the workers to take
 a) plenty of money
 b) their credit cards
 c) an angel on each shoulder
 d) nothing

845. How would the workers be taken care of?

846. Jesus told the workers He was sending them out as
 a) lambs among wolves
 b) cats among dogs
 c) sheep among lions
 d) fish among sharks

847. True or False: When the workers returned to Jesus, they told Him they were amazed by the power Jesus had given them.

Jesus' Resurrection

848. FUNTASTIC FACT! You can read about Jesus' resurrection in all four Gospels. Although all four Gospels don't talk about everything that happened to Jesus, all do record His resurrection. (See Matthew 28:1-15; Mark 16:1-11; Luke 24:1-12; John 20:1-18.)

849. Who were the three women who went to Jesus' grave the day He arose?

850. When the women saw the grave, they discovered that the covering of the grave had been rolled back by
    a) an angel of the Lord
    b) Goliath
    c) Jesus
    d) Samson

851. The one who rolled the stone back told the women,
    a) "You will be punished for stealing the body."
    b) "Expect an earthquake."
    c) "Fear not, for Jesus has risen."
    d) "I'm tired from all that work and I want something to eat."

852. True or False: Jesus' disciples believed the women when they told them that Jesus had risen from the dead.

853. Who went to the grave to see if what the women said was true?

854. True or False: Jesus appeared to Mary Magdalene after He arose.

855. When Jesus saw His disciples after He had risen, He said,
    a) "See, I told you so!"
    b) "Is there any bread left over from the
       Last Supper?"
    c) "Peace be unto you."
    d) "I really missed you these past three days."

856. Jesus said this because He
    a) wanted to show He was right
    b) was hungry
    c) wanted to reassure them
    d) was glad to be back

STEPHEN: THE FIRST MARTYR

857. True or False: Anyone who is persecuted for any reason will be blessed.

858. According to Jesus, what group of people was persecuted in the past? (Hint: Elijah belonged to this group of people.)

859. In what book of the Bible can we read about Stephen?

860. True or False: Stephen was an evil man.

861. FUNTASTIC FACT! Did you know that blasphemy was a serious charge in Stephen's time? The penalty for blasphemy was death. Blasphemy is the act of showing great disrespect for God.

862. Stephen's enemies charged him with
   a) blasphemy
   b) singing off-key in the church choir
   c) selling lottery tickets
   d) charging too much for sacrificial doves

863. True or False: The charges against Stephen were true.

864. During Stephen's trial, he looked
   a) like a guilty prisoner
   b) bored
   c) like an angel
   d) angry

865. Stephen answered the charge against him by
   a) suing his accusers for ruining his reputation
   b) vowing to murder his enemies
   c) throwing a fit
   d) giving a speech in defense of Christianity

866. True or False: Stephen praised Israel during his court appearance.

867. After he spoke, Stephen saw
   a) a large Bible in the sky
   b) the Red Sea part
   c) the glory of God and Jesus at God's right
      hand in heaven
   d) doves

868. How do we know this is what Stephen saw?

869. When the court heard Stephen's speech, they were
    a) angry
    b) afraid
    c) speechless
    d) so emotional, they dropped the charges

870. True or False: Stephen asked God to forgive the people who punished him.

ALL ABOUT LOVE

◇◇◇◇◇◇◇◇◇◇◇◇◇◇◇◇◇◇◇◇◇◇◇◇◇◇◇◇

871. Who wrote 1 Corinthians?

872. The Corinthians who received the letter were
    a) members of the Corinthian Country Club
    b) members of the church at Corinth
    c) makers of Corinthian leather
    d) reporters for the news

873. FUNTASTIC FACT! Did you know that in some older versions of the Bible, the word *charity* is used in place of the word *love* in Paul's first letter to the Corinthians? If you have ever heard someone speak of showing another person Christian charity, it means showing kindness and compassion.

874. True or False: Fine preaching makes up for a lack of love.

875. **True or False:** You don't need love if you have lots of money and faith.

876. **When Paul says love is not puffed up, he means love is not**
    a) fat
    b) filled with air
    c) inflated like a blowfish
    d) proud

877. **What does Paul mean when he says that love is not easily provoked (1 Corinthians 13:5)?**

878. **True or False:** We know everything there is to know while we live on earth.

879. **Of faith, hope, and love, which is the greatest?**

THE FRUIT OF THE SPIRIT

880. **The fruit of the Spirit is**
    a) an orange
    b) a lemon
    c) a set of attitudes you'll have if you love God
    d) the title of a Dr. Seuss book

881. **Where in the Bible can we learn about the fruit of the Spirit?**

882. **Who told us about the fruit of the Spirit?**

883. The Galatians were
a) members of a group of churches in Galatia
b) a galaxy of stars
c) bugs from a popular video game
d) aliens from another galaxy

884. FUNTASTIC FACT! You cannot find Galatia on a modern-day map. Galatia was the name of a region in Asia Minor—modern-day Turkey.

885. One fruit of the Spirit is love. Can you name at least one other letter where Paul writes about love?

886. When Paul speaks of joy, he means
a) a dishwashing detergent
b) happiness in the Lord
c) a baby kangaroo
d) Joseph's nickname

887. FUNTASTIC FACT! There is more than one type of peace. You can be at peace with yourself, which means you like yourself. You can be at peace with others, which means you aren't fighting with anyone. On a national level, this means the country is not at war with another country. Most importantly, you can be at peace with the Lord. This does not mean you are perfect. When you are saved, you know the Lord has forgiven your sins. This puts you at peace with Him.

888. You are long-suffering when
a) you can sit through math class without falling asleep
b) you can do five hundred crunches in a row
c) you can forgive other people when they sin against you
d) you will eat vegetables three meals in a row

889. Paul names "gentleness" as a fruit of the Spirit (Galatians 5:23). Who is the most gentle person you know? What is he or she like?

890. True or False: Goodness is a fruit of the Spirit.

891. True or False: A person of faith must see something to believe it.

892. True or False: Paul wrote about the fruit of the Spirit because he wanted everybody to live by the letter of the Mosaic law.

893. Paul says that those living with the fruit of the Spirit have crucified the flesh. This means they
    a) have Christian tattoos
    b) have pierced their ears
    c) have skin as wrinkled as a prune
    d) don't think about their bodies as much as they think about living for Christ

894. When we walk in the Spirit, it means that
    a) we obey Christ
    b) a cloud surrounds us
    c) we play basketball in high-heeled Easy Spirit pumps
    d) Mom won't drive us to soccer practice

895. True or False: It is all right to be jealous of other people.

896. Why is it important to obey Christ?

897. Now that you have learned about the fruit of the Spirit, can you name all nine?

A LETTER TO THE EPHESIANS

898. True or False: Paul, the writer of Ephesians, always felt a special fondness for Christians and was kind to them all his life.

899. The Ephesians were
   a) weird pizza toppings
   b) members of a baseball team, Ephesus Errors
   c) members of the church at Ephesus
   d) rich people who gave money to Paul's
      political party

900. FUNTASTIC FACT! Ephesus was a city in the Roman province of Asia Minor. Today Asia Minor is part of modern Turkey. (Find Turkey on a map or globe.)

901. How do we know Paul wrote the letter to the Ephesians?

902. True or False: In this letter, Paul says he considers himself the greatest of Jesus' servants.

903. The mystery Paul writes of in Ephesians is that
   a) he is the author of Nancy Drew mysteries
   b) he never misses a good detective show
   c) Gentiles and Jews are equal
   d) Jesus died only for the Gentiles

904. True or False: In Ephesians, Paul reminds us that we all worship one God because all other gods are false.

905. When Paul refers to saints, he means
   a) only those who have died
   b) people who have helped him in the past
   c) an NFL football team
   d) Christians

906. Ephesians includes the instruction to speak the truth in love (Ephesians 4:15). What does this mean?

THE ARMOR OF GOD

907. FUNTASTIC FACT! With the armor of God, you can stand firm against your enemy (Ephesians 6:11)!

Match the piece of armor with what it represents:
   908. breastplate
   909. helmet
   910. shoes
   911. belt
   912. sword of the Spirit
   913. shield

   a) Word of God
   b) salvation
   c) righteousness
   d) gospel of peace
   e) faith
   f) truth

TeACHeRS

914. What husband and wife who were friends with Paul taught Apollos the way of God more accurately?

915. Gamaliel was a famous teacher in the days of Jesus. Which apostle did Gamaliel teach?

916. When Samuel's mother dedicated him to the Lord, who taught him?

917. Besides Paul, who taught Timothy about faith?
   a) his grandma and his mom
   b) his uncle and his brother
   c) his cousins
   d) friendly trolls

918. According to Titus 2:3-5, whom are the older women in the church to teach?

919. Who did Jesus say was the one teacher?

920. Who said to Jesus, "We know that You are a teacher come from God"?

CHURCHeS

921. In what church were the disciples first called Christians?

922. Who were the leaders at the church of Corinth that Paul stayed with?

923. What church was Lydia a part of?
    a) Philippi
    b) Antioch
    c) Thyatira
    d) Corinth

924. What did the apostles appoint in every church?

925. True or False: Barnabas was part of the church at Antioch.

926. Which church sent Paul and Barnabas on their first missionary journey?

CHURCHES IN REVELATION

927. Put the churches in the order they were written to:
    ___Smyrna
    ___Sardis
    ___Ephesus
    ___Thyatira
    ___Laodicea
    ___Pergamum
    ___Philadelphia

928. Which church was told it had left its first love?

929. Which church was told it was lukewarm?

930. Which church was told that they had a Jezebel among them?

931. Which church was told they dwell where Satan's throne is?

932. Which church was told they are alive but dead?

APOSTLES

933. **FUNTASTIC FACT!** *Apostle* means "sent one."

934. Which of the following was not an apostle?
   a) Paul
   b) Peter
   c) Matthias
   d) John Mark

935. How were the apostles distinguished from other people?

936. In the future, what will be the relationship of the apostles to the twelve tribes of Israel?

937. On the day of Pentecost, which apostle preached the sermon?

938. Peter was sent to preach to Cornelius, who was a
   a) Gentile
   b) devout man
   c) centurion
   d) all of the above

939. True or False: The twelve apostles in Acts are the same twelve disciples that Jesus picked.

940. What did Jesus say would be done to the apostles that had been done to the prophets?

941. What did the new members of the church continue in?
    a) the apostles' doctrine
    b) the apostles' fellowship
    c) the apostles' practices
    d) a & b

942. What did the early Christians lay at the apostles' feet?
    a) cookies
    b) skateboards
    c) new clothes
    d) all the material things they wanted to share

943. True or False: When the church at Jerusalem was scattered because of persecution, the apostles were scattered also.

944. Who brought Paul to the apostles?

945. True or False: Barnabas was an apostle.

946. How did Paul become an apostle?

947. Fill in the blank: Paul said he was the chief of sinners (1 Timothy 1:15) and the _____ of the apostles.

948. True or False: Jesus is an apostle.

949. True or False: Peter and Paul had a confrontation.

1 PETER

950. First Peter is a letter written by
   a) Peter
   b) Paul
   c) Mary
   d) Moses

951. True or False: The author of 1 Peter was one of Jesus' apostles.

952. Some scholars think that Peter was the leader of the apostles because he
   a) liked to write letters
   b) is named first in every list of the apostles in the Bible
   c) had the most money
   d) was the only one with Wi-Fi

953. Peter wrote this letter to
   a) Jesus
   b) persecuted Christians
   c) rich Christians
   d) a woman who wanted to publish his life story

954. In 1 Peter 1:4, Peter speaks of an inheritance, meaning that the people he writes to will have
   a) their fortunes told
   b) more money in the future
   c) bodyguards
   d) eternal life

955. True or False: Peter says that when we live like Jesus, we will not live like the rest of the world lives.

956. What does the word *redeemed* mean?

957. Peter says we were redeemed by
   a) Jesus
   b) silver
   c) gift cards
   d) the good things we do for others

958. Peter says that Christians should be like
   a) newborn babies
   b) goats
   c) sheep without a shepherd
   d) Superman

959. The milk of the Word will
   a) taste sour
   b) turn to yogurt
   c) spill on your books
   d) make Christians grow

960. Peter says that Christians are like
   a) cheese
   b) butterflies
   c) living stones
   d) wood

961. True or False: Christians are building a spiritual house.

962. True or False: The name Peter means "rock."

963. Fill in the blank: Jesus is the chief corner____.

964. What does Peter mean when he says that Jesus is the stone of stumbling and rock of offense (1 Peter 2:8)?

965. True or False: It is important for Christians to live as Christ wants because the world is watching us.

966. Peter calls Christians *sojourners* (1 Peter 2:11 ESV). What is a sojourner?

967. Christians should
    a) disobey all laws made by men
    b) obey the laws of their nations
    c) fight against the law
    d) obey the laws they think are right

968. True or False: It is all right to be mean to someone who is mean to you first.

969. When people say mean things to us, we should
    a) remember how Jesus trusted God
    b) gossip about them
    c) take them to court and let the judge decide
       what to do
    d) tell the teacher

970. Peter compares the Christians to
    a) blocks of wood
    b) diamonds
    c) lost sheep
    d) all of the above

971. Peter refers to Jesus as a shepherd. What famous psalm also says He is a shepherd?

972. True or False: Christian women should depend completely on lipstick, perfume, and jewels to make them pretty.

973. True or False: Those who suffer because they are Christians are blessed.

974. Peter says that Christians should answer questions about the Christian faith with
    a) anger
    b) meekness
    c) a funny greeting card
    d) an email message

975. FUNTASTIC FACT! When Peter says, "Love covers a multitude of sins" (1 Peter 4:8 ESV), this is a quote from Proverbs 10:12.

976. True or False: Peter says that Christians should rejoice at being tested because they share in suffering with Christ.

977. Young people should submit to their
    a) impulse to play computer games all day
    b) elders
    c) sisters
    d) friends at school

978. Who is the enemy of Christians?

2 PETER

979. **FUNTASTIC FACT!** Second Peter was written in AD 66, one year after 1 Peter was written.

980. **Peter wrote his second letter to**
    a) Christians in Asia Minor
    b) Christians in the United States
    c) Jews in Israel
    d) his fifth-grade class

981. **True or False:** Peter says we are more like Jesus when we give up worldly things.

982. **Peter lists eight traits that a Christian should have. One of these is faith. Can you name the others?**

983. **FUNTASTIC FACT!** Peter was probably over seventy years old and in a Roman prison when he wrote this letter.

984. **True or False:** Peter was an eyewitness to God's confirmation that Jesus is the Messiah.

985. **True or False:** God will spare false prophets.

986. **False prophets**
    a) lie
    b) disrespect God
    c) tell people what they want to hear
    d) all of the above

987. The day of the Lord will arrive
   a) as fast as a pizza delivery guy
   b) as a thief in the night
   c) as soon as the circus comes to town
   d) absolutely, positively on July 7, 2077

988. True or False: Peter warns Christians not to fall away from the faith.

989. Why is it important for us to study Peter's letters?

SIN
◇◇◇◇

990. If we say we have no sin, we are fooling
   a) ourselves
   b) our parents
   c) our teachers
   d) our friends

991. Fill in the blank: Romans 6:23 says the wages of sin is _____.

992. What colors did Isaiah use to describe sin?

993. Fill in the blank: God said He would make our sin as white as _____.
   a) snow
   b) wool
   c) a swan
   d) a & b

994. According to Psalm 103:12, how far has God removed our sin from us?

    a) as far as north is from south

    b) as far as east is from west

    c) as far as heaven is from hell

    d) as far as the earth is from the sun

995. When does God forgive us our sins and cleanse us from all unrighteousness?

SALVATION

996. Fill in the blank: "The LORD is my light and my _____."

997. To receive salvation, we have to pay Jesus

    a) by being pastors or missionaries when we grow up whether we want to or not

    b) by spending at least an hour a day reading the Bible

    c) by ignoring people who tease us

    d) with nothing; His gift of salvation is free

998. What is the one requirement Jesus gives for receiving eternal life (salvation)?

999. Fill in the blanks: "Because, if you confess with your _____ that Jesus is Lord and believe in your _____ that God raised him from the dead, you will be saved."

ANSWER KEY

2. sixty-six

3. False; thirty-nine

4. True

5.
Genesis
Exodus
Leviticus
Numbers
Deuteronomy
Joshua
Judges
Ruth
1 Samuel
2 Samuel
1 Kings
2 Kings
1 Chronicles
2 Chronicles
Ezra
Nehemiah
Esther
Job
Psalms
Proverbs
Ecclesiastes
Song of Solomon

Isaiah
Jeremiah
Lamentations
Ezekiel
Daniel
Hosea
Joel
Amos
Obadiah
Jonah
Micah
Nahum
Habakkuk
Zephaniah
Haggai
Zechariah
Malachi

6.
Matthew
Mark
Luke
John
Acts
Romans
1 Corinthians
2 Corinthians
Galatians
Ephesians
Philippians
Colossians
1 Thessalonians
2 Thessalonians

1 Timothy
2 Timothy
Titus
Philemon
Hebrews
James
1 Peter
2 Peter
1 John
2 John
3 John
Jude
Revelation

7. *Testament* means "covenant" or "contract," which is a serious agreement that can be trusted.

9. b) Moses

10. d) Paul

12. c) Hebrew, Aramaic, and Greek

13. a) John Wycliffe; in 1382

14. c) 1454. The Bible was first printed by Johannes Gutenberg.

15. Psalms

16. 2 John

17. Psalm 119

18. Psalm 117

19. Esther 8:9

20. John 11:35

21. d) Pentateuch

22. Moses

23. a) creation of the universe

24. twelve

25. Gad, Dan, Naphtali

26. a) God gave the laws to Moses

27. These records are important to show family lineage. Because of these records, we can trace Jesus' family line back to Adam and Eve.

28. False. We don't know who wrote several books, including Job, 1 and 2 Samuel, 1 and 2 Kings, or Esther.

29. b) four hundred. This is called the "intertestamental" period, or the silent years. During this time, society changed so that the New Testament world was much different from the Old Testament world. This explains why the New Testament was written in different languages and reflects different customs.

30. False. Israel was no longer an independent nation but a province of a larger empire.

31. Matthew, Mark, Luke, and John

32. a) the life and ministry of Jesus

33. False (2 Timothy 3:16). God speaks to us through all the books of the Bible. We must know His entire Word to be faithful.

34. d) all of the above

35. c) a letter

36. anyone who is not a Jew

37. c) Paul the apostle

38. Acts

39. c) love one another, behave, and conduct church business

40. Even though they were written almost 2,000 years ago, the instructions contained in Paul's letters are still timely. For example, we should always love one another. How we present ourselves as individual people and as members of a church is a witness for Christ. The world watches us. We must live as Christ wants us to live—and Paul tells us how.

41. a) love (1 Corinthians 13:1-13)

42. True

43. Revelation

44. Genesis 1

45. "In the beginning" (Genesis 1:1 KJV)

46. c) six (Genesis 1:31–2:3)

47. a) seed-bearing plants and fruit (Genesis 1:29)

48. "very good" (Genesis 1:31 ESV)

49. alone (Genesis 2:18 NIV)

50. light, skies and seas, plants and flowers and trees, sun and moon and stars, birds and fish, animals and man, rest (Genesis 1–2:3)

51. Moses

52. He separated day and night (Genesis 1:3–5).

53. the sun, the moon, and the stars (Genesis 1:14–19)

55. c) to water the garden (Genesis 2:10)

56. d) Adam

57. Adam (Genesis 2:19)

58. c) Eve

60. a rib (Genesis 2:21)

62. c) serpent

63. d) knowledge of good and evil

64. They sewed themselves aprons made of fig leaves (Genesis 3:7 KJV).

65. They hid themselves (Genesis 3:8).

66. d) Eve (Genesis 3:12)

67. a) sent them out of Eden (Genesis 3:22-24)

68. c) cherubim (Genesis 3:24)

69. in the middle (Genesis 2:9)

70. the tree of knowledge of good and evil (Genesis 2:9 KJV)

71. the tree of life (Genesis 2:9)

72. one (Genesis 2:10)

73. d) thorns and thistles (Genesis 3:17-18)

74. guardians of Eden and the tree of life (Genesis 3:24)

75. a) Genesis. The story is told in chapters 6-9.

76. False. God was angry that the people were so evil (Genesis 6:5-6).

77. c) righteous (Genesis 6:9)

78. Shem, Ham, and Japheth (Genesis 6:10)

79. d) one hundred (Genesis 5:32; 7:11)

80. c) gopher wood (Genesis 6:14 KJV)

82. c) 600 years old (Genesis 7:6)

83. favor (Genesis 6:8 ESV)

84. forty days and forty nights (Genesis 7:12)

86. a) seven and a half months. The flood began on the seventeenth day of the second month (Genesis 7:11). And Noah was able to see the tops of the mountains again on the first day of the tenth month (Genesis 8:5).

87. raven (Genesis 8:7)

88. d) a dove (Genesis 8:8)

89. d) an olive branch (Genesis 8:11). This showed Noah that the water had started to go down.

90. c) built an altar to God and made sacrifices upon it (Genesis 8:20)

91. b) planted a vineyard (Genesis 9:20)

92. True (Genesis 8:21; 9:11)

93. a rainbow (Genesis 9:13)

94. d) 950 (Genesis 9:29)

96. True (Genesis 11:1)

97. d) an unspecified language. Everyone spoke the same language (Genesis 11:1), but the Bible does not say what language the people spoke.

98. c) brick (Genesis 11:3)

99. True (Genesis 11:4-5)

100. d) reach to heaven (Genesis 11:4)

101. False (Genesis 11:6-7)

102. d) made the people all speak different languages so they couldn't finish the work (Genesis 11:7)

103. The story of the Tower of Babel is important because:
1. It shows us that God places limits upon mankind (Genesis 11:6).
2. It explains why we speak different languages (Genesis 11:6-9).
3. It shows how God scattered the people all over the face of the earth (Genesis 11:9).

104. True

105. Genesis 17

106. True (Genesis 17:5)

107. c) ninety-nine (Genesis 17:1)

108. c) obey Him (Genesis 17:1)

109. b) bowed down, touching his face to the ground (Genesis 17:3)

111. True (Genesis 17:2)

112. a) a relative of a future generation

113. d) the land of Canaan (Genesis 17:8). Abraham was living in Canaan as a foreigner at that time.

114. True. The covenant applied to Abraham and to future generations as well (Genesis 17:8).

115. c) Abraham was to be the father of many nations (Genesis 17:5)

116. True (Genesis 17:6)

117. True (Genesis 17:7)

118. Abraham's wife was named Sarai before God renamed her Sarah (Genesis 17:15).

119. c) have a baby (Genesis 17:16)

120. b) laughed (Genesis 17:17). Abraham did not think it was possible for him and his wife to be new parents because they were so old.

121. a baby boy (Genesis 17:16)

122. c) was ninety years old, which is usually too old to have a baby (Genesis 17:17)

123. ninety-nine years old (Genesis 17:1)

124. c) a person who receives an inheritance. In biblical times, the firstborn son usually was next in line for his father's position and money when the father died. This meant that after the father died, the oldest son became head of the family.

125. False (Genesis 17:19-21)

126. Like Abraham, Christians are people of God. We are Abraham's descendants.

128. b) he would die from hunger and would have no use for it (Genesis 25:32)

129. a bowl of stew (Genesis 25:29-34)

130. the skins of young goats (Genesis 27:16)

131. a) he would be the father of kings (Genesis 35:11-12)

132. True (Genesis 32:27-28; 35:9-10)

133. Rebekah, Isaac's wife (Genesis 25:20-26)

134. d) hunt (Genesis 25:27)

135. a) servant (Genesis 33:5)

137. water to blood, frogs, lice, flies, diseased live-stock, boils, hail and fire, locusts, darkness, death of firstborn

138. they died (Exodus 7:21)

139. seven days (Exodus 7:25)

140. three: rod to snake (Exodus 7:12), water to blood (Exodus 7:21–22), frogs (Exodus 8:7)

141. lice (Exodus 8:16 KJV)

142. three days (Exodus 10:22)

143. True (Exodus 10:23)

144. the land of Goshen where God's people lived (Exodus 8:22)

145. handfuls of ashes from a furnace (Exodus 9:8–9)

146. c) they were covered in boils (Exodus 9:11)

147. into the Red Sea (Exodus 10:19)

149. gods (Exodus 20:3 ESV)

150. image (Exodus 20:4 ESV)

151. vain (Exodus 20:7 ESV)

152. holy (Exodus 20:8 ESV)

153. father, mother (Exodus 20:12 ESV)

154. murder (Exodus 20:13 ESV)

155. adultery (Exodus 20:14 ESV)

156. steal (Exodus 20:15 ESV)

157. witness (Exodus 20:16 ESV)

158. covet (Exodus 20:17 ESV)

159. a) Leviticus

160. b) Mount Sinai (Exodus 19:20)

161. b) been brought out of slavery in Egypt

162. b) stone tablets (Deuteronomy 5:22)

164. False. The second commandment tells us not to make any idols (Exodus 20:4; Deuteronomy 5:8–9).

165. God means we are not to call His name unless we are praying to Him or worshipping Him. Think about how you would feel if people kept saying your name, attracting your attention for no reason. Would you feel angry? Would you be upset? God does not want us to call His name unless we mean to speak to Him or to praise His name.

166. d) keep holy, cease work, and remember His people's deliverance from Egypt (Exodus 20:8–11; Deuteronomy 5:12–15)

167. God wants us to rest every seventh day because He rested on the seventh day after He created the world (Exodus 20:11). By resting on the seventh day, we are honoring God by being like Him in this way.

168. We can find out how God established marriage in Genesis 2:21–34.

169. d) wish we had our neighbor's stuff. Do you know someone who would like something you have, such as an iPad or a bike? Why not share it with that person? You may make a new friend.

170. False. While Moses was with God on the mountain for forty days, the people made a false idol. Moses was so angry with their disobedience to God, he broke the tablets when he came down the mountain (Deuteronomy 9:17).

173. The ark of the covenant was a wooden box covered with gold and built to God's specification. It contained the stone tablets on which the Ten Commandments were written.

174. gold (Exodus 25:13)

175. False. Moses inspected the work after it was built (Exodus 39:43).

176. Levi (Deuteronomy 10:8 ESV)

177. He fell backward off his chair, broke his neck, and died (1 Samuel 4:18).

178. b) oxen pulling the cart carrying it stumbled (2 Samuel 6:6)

179. d) Solomon (1 Kings 8:12, 17–21)

180. Most Holy Place (Hebrews 9:2–4)

181. c) Aaron's staff that had budded (Hebrews 9:4)

182. in heaven (Revelation 11:19)

183. the apostle John (Revelation 11:19)

184. b) Sinai (Exodus 25:16–22)

186. True (Numbers 27:18–23)

187. c) the death of Moses

188. Joshua

189. c) Jordan River (Joshua 1:2)

190. c) the home of a wicked woman (Joshua 2:1)

191. True (Joshua 2:2–7)

193. a) on the roof (Joshua 2:6)

195. True (Joshua 2:10–14)

196. Rahab protected the spies because she knew they were there to claim the land for the Lord's people (Joshua 2:9).

198. forty thousand (Joshua 4:13)

199. b) eaten food grown in the Promised Land (Joshua 5:11)

200. Manna was the food God rained down upon the Israelites to provide food for them while they were wandering in the wilderness on their way to the Promised Land. God rained fresh manna for them every day (Exodus 16:14–18).

201. False. The walls came tumbling down by the sounds of horns and a shout. The priests blew horns for seven days as they walked around the city with the ark of the covenant (Joshua 6:3–16).

202. The lives of Rahab and her household were spared during the fall of Jericho. This is important because it shows God always keeps His promises (Joshua 6:17, 22–23).

203. b) put into the Lord's treasury (Joshua 6:19)

204. True (Joshua 6:27)

205. in the book of Judges

207. False. Deborah was an exception.

208. d) prophet (Judges 4:4)

209. False (Judges 4:1)

210. a) made life very hard for the Israelites (Judges 4:3)

211. nine hundred (Judges 4:3)

212. They were slaves to King Jabin for twenty years (Judges 4:3).

213. They were doing "evil in the eyes of the LORD" (Judges 4:1 NIV). Though God punishes those who do evil, He also forgives those who ask for forgiveness and repent of their sins.

214. True (Judges 4:6)

215. c) deliver the enemy into the hands of Israel's general (Judges 4:6–7)

216. Mount Tabor was located in Galilee, on the borders of Naphtali and Zebulun. Some of the men in the army who were to defeat Sisera were from Naphtali and Zebulun.

217. c) a general in Israel's army (Judges 4:6–7)

218. a) Deborah, to ensure success. Deborah had already proposed taking 10,000 men, but Barak was afraid of defeat, even with such a large army (Judges 4:8).

219. b) a woman (Judges 4:9)

220. False. Men were the heads of Jewish households. Women could not speak for themselves in legal matters. Women were spoken for by their fathers, husbands, sons, or closest male relative.

221. Yes (Judges 4:16)

222. a) the fifth chapter of Judges

224. Judges

225. False (Judges 14:3)

226. a) his bare hands (Judges 14:5-6)

227. honey (Judges 14:8)

228. b) burned the Philistines' corn (Judges 15:1-10)

229. the Spirit of the Lord loosed the bonds (Judges 15:14)

230. False. He killed them with a donkey's jawbone (Judges 15:15).

231. d) carried away the city gate (Judges 16:2-3)

232. the source of his strength (Judges 16:5)

233. True (Judges 16:5)

234. razor, shaved (Judges 16:17 ESV)

235. False. The Philistines praised their own god (Judges 16:24).

236. strengthen (Judges 16:28 ESV)

237. a) destroyed the pillars of a crowded house, causing its collapse (Judges 16:29–30)

238. True (Judges 16:30)

240. a) judges (Ruth 1:1)

241. Four people went to Moab: Naomi, her husband, and her two sons, who were unmarried at the time (Ruth 1:1-2).

242. Bethlehem, in Judah (Ruth 1:1)

243. False (Ruth 1:3-4)

244. Mahlon and Chilion (Ruth 1:2)

245. c) she couldn't bear more sons for them to marry (Ruth 1:11)

246. a) Mara, meaning "bitter" (Ruth 1:20)

247. barley (Ruth 1:22)

248. False. He welcomed her to glean in his field and instructed his young men not to touch her (Ruth 2:7-9).

249. False. She told Ruth to go see Boaz at night at the threshing floor (Ruth 3:1-3).

250. c) said she would do as Naomi instructed (Ruth 3:5)

251. False. Boaz was not the nearest kinsman-redeemer, so first he had to find out if that man wanted to marry Ruth before he could propose marriage (Ruth 3:9-13).

252. c) took off his shoe (Ruth 4:7-8). This action signaled that the contract was sealed.

253. a) seven sons (Ruth 4:14-15)

254. Obed was the father of Jesse, who was the father of David. Ruth, a Moabitess, was part of the lineage of Jesus Christ (Matthew 1:5-16).

255. b) he was taking food to his brothers. David's three older brothers were soldiers in battle (1 Samuel 17:17).

257. False. Goliath wore bronze armor all over his body. A soldier went before him to carry his shield. Goliath carried a large spear (1 Samuel 17:5-7).

258. False. They were too scared to fight Goliath (1 Samuel 17:11).

259. b) tended sheep (1 Samuel 17:15)

260. True (1 Samuel 17:23)

262. False. Eliab, the oldest, scolded David and asked him who was tending his sheep (1 Samuel 17:28).

263. a) wondered how Goliath dared to defy the army of the living God (1 Samuel 17:26)

264. forty (1 Samuel 17:16)

265. c) was only a boy (1 Samuel 17:33)

267. True (1 Samuel 17:36)

268. c) he couldn't walk in it because he wasn't used to such bulky armor (1 Samuel 17:39)

269. five (1 Samuel 17:40)

270. False. Goliath made fun of David (1 Samuel 17:43–44).

271. d) there is a God in Israel (1 Samuel 17:46)

272. True. The stone hit his forehead and Goliath fell facedown to the ground (1 Samuel 17:49).

273. a) chased the Philistines back to their own country (1 Samuel 17:52)

274. the Old Testament

275. d) Sheba (1 Kings 10:1; 2 Chronicles 9:1)

276. a) she had heard of his fame (1 Kings 10:1; 2 Chronicles 9:1)

278. True (1 Kings 10:1; 2 Chronicles 9:1)

279. d) unknown; her questions are not recorded in the Bible. Some scholars believe they may have been puzzling riddles designed to stump Solomon.

280. a) wisdom and sacrifices to God (1 Kings 10:4–5; 2 Chronicles 9:3–4)

281. c) riches, palace, food, and servants (1 Kings 10:4–5; 2 Chronicles 9:3–4)

282. False. The queen told Solomon she was amazed that he possessed twice as much wisdom as she had been told (1 Kings 10:7; 2 Chronicles 9:6).

283. True (1 Kings 10:9; 2 Chronicles 9:8)

284. Because she was from a foreign land, it is assumed the queen of Sheba worshipped pagan gods rather than the God of Israel. When she saw Solomon's riches and heard his wisdom, she considered him blessed by God, causing her to praise Him. Christians today are witnesses for Jesus Christ. However, Jesus asks us to live a life of love and forgiveness under His grace rather than displaying vast wealth.

286. The total is 9,000 pounds.

287. a) 1 Kings (17:1)

288. c) a prophet

289. True (1 Kings 17:1)

290. d) no rain for the next few years until God commanded rain to fall (1 Kings 17:1)

291. God was angry with King Ahab because he was evil (1 Kings 16:30).

292. False (1 Kings 16:30)

293. b) worshipped the god Baal (1 Kings 16:31-32)

294. a) Elijah's prophecy had made King Ahab mad

295. a) ravens (1 Kings 17:4)

296. d) bread and meat in the morning and evening (1 Kings 17:6). The Bible does not tell us what kind of bread and meat the ravens brought.

297. b) a widow (1 Kings 17:9)

298. The brook dried up because, as God had promised, there was no rain (1 Kings 17:7).

299. False (1 Kings 17:12-14)

300. d) prayed to God (1 Kings 17:21). This is the same widow who had fed Elijah while he was in hiding.

301. True (1 Kings 17:23)

302. b) stretching himself out on the boy three times (1 Kings 17:19–22)

303. twelve stones (1 Kings 18:31–32)

304. Baal (1 Kings 18:22, 40)

305. False (1 Kings 19:11–12)

306. d) all of the above (Matthew 16:14). This answer (see also Mark 8:28; Luke 9:19) given by Jesus' disciples shows there was confusion about Jesus. Since He healed people and performed miracles, some thought Jesus was one of the prophets risen from the dead. The confusion is especially evident when you remember that Jesus was born six months *after* John the Baptist (Luke 1:41) and was baptized by him (Matthew 3:13; Mark 1:9). Since they lived on earth at the same time, there is no way Jesus could have been John the Baptist. The disciples knew who Jesus was, however. We are to remember Peter's answer: "Thou art the Christ, the Son of the living God" (Matthew 16:16 KJV).

307. True. This miracle of God is called the transfiguration (Matthew 17:1–3).

308. The disciples answer this with a question they asked Jesus: "Why then do the teachers of the law say that Elijah must come first?" (Matthew 17:10 NIV). The return of Elijah, a revered Old Testament prophet, was to signal the coming of the Jewish Messiah.

309. True. These are Jesus' own words: "But I say unto you, That Elias is come already, and they knew him not, but have done unto him whatsoever they listed" (Matthew 17:12 KJV). This means John the Baptist was the Elijah, but the people did not recognize him.

311. a) whirlwind (2 Kings 2:11)

312. a) a cloak (2 Kings 2:9-13)

313. False (1 Kings 19:19)

314. b) 2 Kings

315. False

316. True (2 Kings 2:9)

317. b) dividing the Jordan River and walking on dry land (2 Kings 2:14). He struck the water with Elijah's cloak, and the water parted.

318. True (2 Kings 2:15)

319. c) made the water pure (2 Kings 2:20-22)

320. c) bald (2 Kings 2:23)

321. b) bears (2 Kings 2:23-24)

322. c) rebelled against Israel (2 Kings 3:5)

323. True (2 Kings 3:16)

324. c) they thought the water they saw around the camp was blood (2 Kings 3:21–23). When the Moabites saw water on what had been dry land, they thought it was blood because the sunlight hit it in such a way that the water appeared to be red. They thought the three armies had killed each other, so they decided to rob the camp.

325. They were attacked by the Israelites (2 Kings 3:24).

326. True (2 Kings 3:24–25)

327. a) was in debt (2 Kings 4:1)

328. d) a small jar of olive oil (2 Kings 4:2). Elisha told her to get jars from her neighbors and pour the oil into them (2 Kings 4:3).

329. The woman poured the small amount of olive oil she had in her house into all the jars. When they were all filled, the oil stopped.

330. a) oil (2 Kings 4:1–7)

331. True (2 Kings 4:7). She sold the oil for money.

332. No, she did not accept his offer (2 Kings 4:13).

333. b) promising her that she would have a baby (2 Kings 4:17). The woman was rich, but she had no son. She gave birth to a baby boy as Elisha had promised.

334. c) setting up a room for him to stay in when he visited (2 Kings 4:10)

335. True (2 Kings 4:18–37)

336. a) brought the boy back from the dead (2 Kings 4:18–37)

338. True. There had been a famine, so food was scarce. The cook used poisonous gourds by mistake. Elisha made the stew pure so they could eat it (2 Kings 4:38–41).

339. False. Naaman was a respected Syrian commander (2 Kings 5:1).

340. a) leprosy (2 Kings 5:1)

341. a servant girl (2 Kings 5:2–3)

342. True (2 Kings 5:8)

343. a) wash seven times in the Jordan River (2 Kings 5:10)

344. b) was angry. He did not understand why he could not wash himself in a river in Damascus and become cured there (2 Kings 5:11).

345. False. Naaman was cured as soon as he rose from bathing in the Jordan River the seventh time (2 Kings 5:14).

346. Elisha's God (2 Kings 5:18)

347. d) two mule loads (2 Kings 5:17)

349. b) Gehazi (2 Kings 5:20)

350. True (2 Kings 5:22)

351. Yes. Naaman gave Gehazi six thousand pieces of silver rather than the three thousand he asked for, plus the two changes of clothes that Gehazi requested (2 Kings 5:23).

352. False. Elisha rebuked him for his greed (2 Kings 5:26).

353. d) said that Gehazi and his family would always be plagued with leprosy (2 Kings 5:27)

354. False. Very few of the kings pleased God.

356. b) worshipped the god Baal (1 Kings 16:31)

357. b) Jezebel (1 Kings 16:31)

358. False. Jezebel was evil and did not influence Ahab to worship the true God, the God of Israel (1 Kings 16:31).

359. True (1 Kings 16:30–33)

360. c) God commanded it to rain (1 Kings 17:1)

361. True (1 Kings 18:20–21)

362. a) it was near his palace and he wanted to use it as a vegetable garden (1 Kings 21:2)

363. a) a better vineyard or to pay him what it was worth (1 Kings 21:2)

364. d) God refused to let him give King Ahab the land (1 Kings 21:3)

365. c) sulked and refused to eat (1 Kings 21:4)

366. True (1 Kings 21:9)

367. Yes (1 Kings 21:14)

368. a) took it (1 Kings 21:16)

369. True (1 Kings 21:19). God is never, ever fooled.

370. Elijah (1 Kings 21:17)

371. True (1 Kings 21:19)

372. b) Manasseh (2 Kings 21:1-3)

374. False. Ezra's name isn't mentioned until chapter 7.

375. b) the end of the Jews' captivity in Babylon

376. King Cyrus of Persia (Ezra 1:2)

377. 49,897 (Ezra 2:64-65)

378. False. Israel's enemies opposed it.

379. False. Because the nation of Israel was not as wealthy as it was during David and Solomon's time, there were not as many materials to build a grand structure.

380. b) Persia

381. No. Though Israel's enemies had opposed the rebuilding of the temple for many years, it was Artaxerxes who put a halt to its construction.

382. c) sending a letter (Ezra 4:8)

384. d) rebellious (Ezra 4:19)

385. Yes. They rebelled once against the Assyrians (2 Kings 18:7) and twice against Babylon (2 Kings 24:1, 20).

386. c) the city not be rebuilt until his command (Ezra 4:21)

387. True (Ezra 4:24)

388. Yes. They were questioned by the governor of the region, who then sent a letter to King Darius (Ezra 5:3-7).

389. b) whatever they needed to make sacrifices to God (Ezra 6:9-10)

391. c) suffering (Nehemiah 1:3)

392. False. The walls had been destroyed, which is why Nehemiah was called upon to undertake building the wall.

393. True (Nehemiah 1:11)

394. a) wept and prayed to God (Nehemiah 1:4–11)

395. b) cupbearer (Nehemiah 1:11). This was an important position that put Nehemiah in the king's presence every day.

396. b) looked sad. Nehemiah had never before looked sad, so the king asked him if he was sick. Nehemiah told the king his people were unhappy (Nehemiah 2:1–3).

397. c) go back and rebuild the city of Jerusalem (Nehemiah 2:5)

398. Yes, the king granted Nehemiah's request (Nehemiah 2:6).

399. True (Nehemiah 2:3)

401. b) his donkey (Nehemiah 2:12)

402. True (Nehemiah 2:19)

403. God (Nehemiah 2:20)

404. d) the sheep gate (Nehemiah 3:1, 32)

405. False. In fact, people tried to stop the work many times. Enemies made fun of the wall builders (Nehemiah 2:19; 4:1-3); they threatened an attack (Nehemiah 4:7-23); enemies tried to distract Nehemiah from the project (Nehemiah 6:1-4); people tried to ruin Nehemiah's reputation (Nehemiah 6:5-9, 10-14); finally, letters were sent to Nehemiah to scare him into stopping the project (Nehemiah 6:17-19).

406. False. He prayed to God, and the enemies' plans to sabotage the project were halted (Nehemiah 4:14-15).

407. a) they were too poor to feed their families (Nehemiah 5:2)

408. c) the rich Jews were taking advantage of their poor relatives (Nehemiah 5:7). They were forcing them to pay high taxes. They also loaned them money to be paid back with interest, a practice that was against the Jewish religion. Some people were so poor that they had to sell themselves into slavery (Nehemiah 5:4-6).

409. True (Nehemiah 5:12)

410. b) shook his sash (Nehemiah 5:13)

411. Yes (Nehemiah 5:13)

412. False. Nehemiah did not tax his people or buy property for himself (Nehemiah 5:15-16).

414. fifty-two (Nehemiah 6:15)

415. two

416. False (Esther 1:12)

417. c) foiling an assassination attempt on the king (Esther 2:21–23)

419. False. He was very proud that he was the only other invited guest, other than the king (Esther 5:12).

420. c) she refused to come when Xerxes sent for her (Esther 1:12)

421. extended his gold scepter to her (Esther 4:11)

422. perish, perish (Esther 4:16 ESV)

423. b) appealed to Esther and fell on her couch (Esther 7:8)

424. one (Jezebel) (1 Kings 16:31)

425. one (Athaliah) (2 Kings 11:1)

426. b) mother and daughter

427. killed all her grandchildren so she could be queen (2 Kings 11:1)

428. Jezebel

430. resolved (Daniel 1:8 ESV)

431. c) ten (Daniel 1:15)

432. True (Daniel 2:48 ESV)

433. a) Darius (Daniel 6:1, 16)

434. b) government leaders (Daniel 6:4)

435. True (Daniel 6:5)

436. True (Daniel 6:7)

437. c) three (Daniel 6:10)

438. False. He did his best to keep Daniel from being thrown into the lions' den (Daniel 6:14).

439. King Darius (Daniel 6:16 NLT)

440. an angel (Daniel 6:22)

441. True (Daniel 6:24)

442. True (Daniel 1:3–4)

443. c) gold (Daniel 3:1)

444. worship (Daniel 3:5)

445. b) Chaldeans (Daniel 3:8–12)

446. Shadrach, Meshach, and Abednego (Daniel 3:16–17 NIV)

447. False. He ordered it heated seven times hotter than normal (Daniel 3:19).

448. b) mighty men (Daniel 3:20)

449. True (Daniel 3:22)

452. the Lord (Jonah 1:1–2)

453. b) the Lord was against their wickedness (Jonah 1:2)

454. b) Tarshish

455. c) he wanted to flee from the Lord (Jonah 1:3)

456. A great wind caused the sea to rage (Jonah 1:4).

457. a great fish (Jonah 1:17)

458. three days and three nights (Jonah 1:17)

459. forty (Jonah 3:4)

460. c) fasted and wore sackcloth (Jonah 3:5)

461. False (Jonah 3:6)

462. a) Nineveh wasn't part of his own country (Jonah 4:2)

463. True (Jonah 4:3)

464. He wanted to see what would happen to the city (Jonah 4:5).

465. b) a worm (Jonah 4:7)

467. fear (Psalm 34:7 ESV)

468. c) wisdom

469. twice (Genesis 22:10–18)

470. c) a donkey (Numbers 22:23)

471. presence

472. True (Exodus 14:19)

473. two (Genesis 19:1)

474. c) "You will run aground." (Acts 27:23-26)

475. a) Samson's father (Judges 13:19-29)

476. c) three; cherubim (Genesis 3:24), seraphim (Isaiah 6:2), archangel (Jude 9)

477. cherubim (Exodus 25:18)

478. We might be entertaining angels unaware.

479. d) a & b (Psalm 91:11-12)

480. Michael (Daniel 10:13)

481. Satan (2 Corinthians 11:14)

482. b) destroy the city (1 Chronicles 21:15)

483. Ezekiel (Ezekiel 10:20)

484. four (Ezekiel 1:6)

485. six (Isaiah 6:2)

486. d) shouted for joy (Job 38:7)

487. around the throne

488. two (Luke 24:4)

489. d) all of the above (Zechariah 4:4-7, 12-14; 5:1-3)

490. two (Acts 1:10-11)

491. one, followed by a multitude (Luke 2:9, 13)

492. True (Matthew 18:10)

493. worship the Lamb who was slain
(Revelation 5:11-12)

494. c) manna

495. Cornelius (Acts 10:3)

497. Christians (1 Corinthians 6:3)

498. c) there will be no more delay

500. c) Egypt (Genesis 12:10)

501. d) the land of the Philistines (Genesis 26)

502. Joseph (Genesis 41:29-30, 56)

503. False; during the days of Elisha (2 Kings 4:38)

504. d) Moab (Ruth 1:1)

505. three (2 Samuel 21:1)

506. True (Acts 11:28)

508. foxes (Judges 15:3-5)

509. ox (Deuteronomy 25:4)

510. animals, reptiles, and birds (Acts 10:9-12)

511. animal skins (Genesis 3:21)

512. ram (Genesis 22:13)

513. donkey (Numbers 22:27-28)

514. deer (Psalm 42:1)

515. donkey (John 12:14-15)

516. lion (Proverbs 30:30)

517. dog (1 Samuel 17:43)

518. dragons (Malachi 1:3 KJV)

519. white, red, black, pale

520. a donkey and a colt (Matthew 21:2)

521. camel (Matthew 19:24)

522. gone astray (Isaiah 53:6 ESV)

523. True (Matthew 18:12–14; Luke 15:4–7)

524. finds (Luke 15:4 ESV)

525. speckled (Genesis 30:32)

526. d) on his shoulders (Luke 15:5)

527. Jesus (John 10:11 ESV)

528. a thief and a robber (John 10:1)

529. shepherd of the sheep (John 10:2 ESV)

530. follow me (John 10:27 ESV)

531. goats (Matthew 25:33)

532. souls (1 Peter 2:25 NKJV)

533. shepherd (Psalm 23:1 ESV)

534. "for you are with me; your rod and your staff, they comfort me" (Psalm 23:4 ESV)

535. Peter (1 Peter 5:4 ESV)

536. c) they thought they were an abomination (Genesis 46:34)

537. Chief, Great, Good (1 Peter 5:4 NIV; Hebrews 13:20; John 10:11)

538. lambs (Isaiah 40:11 ESV)

539. as one who leaves the flock (Zechariah 11:17 NKJV)

540. his disciples (Matthew 26:31 NKJV)

541. day 3 (Genesis 1:12–13)

542. lily of the field (Matthew 6:28–29)

543. the word of the Lord (1 Peter 1:24–25 NKJV)

544. bulrushes (Exodus 2:3)

545. tree of life (Genesis 2:9; Revelation 2:7)

546. the tree of life, the tree of the knowledge of good and evil, fig tree (Genesis 2:9; 3:7)

547. palm (Judges 4:4–5)

548. True (Song of Solomon 2:3 NKJV)

549. clap their hands

550. sycamore (Luke 19:4)

551. d) all of the above (Psalm 104:25 NKJV)

552. d) a & c (Psalm 107:23-24 NKJV)

553. True (Proverbs 8:29)

554. the army of Pharaoh (Exodus 14:28)

555. the knowledge of the glory of the Lord (Habakkuk 2:14 NKJV)

556. glass, crystal (Revelation 4:6 NKJV)

557. True (Revelation 21:1)

558. d) b & c (Numbers 34:11; Luke 5:1)

559. the Salt Sea (Deuteronomy 3:17 NKJV)

560. b) ladder (Genesis 28:10-12)

561. a) cattle (Genesis 41:20)

562. Pharaoh (Genesis 41:5-7)

563. b) Peter (Acts 10:9-13)

564. a) wise men (Matthew 2:1, 12)

565. b) Joseph (Matthew 1:20)

566. d) Pilate's wife (Matthew 27:17–19)

567. c) four (Daniel 7:3)

568. False; sheaves (Genesis 37:7)

569. Jacob rebuked him (Genesis 37:10)

570. two (Genesis 37:5–11)

571. jail (Genesis 40:1–3)

572. c) a round loaf of barley bread overturned it (Judges 7:13)

573. c) the wife of Pilate (Matthew 27:19)

574. d) all of the above (Daniel 2:2)

575. b) Nebuchadnezzar would not tell them the contents of the dream (Daniel 2:1–9)

576. Moses (Deuteronomy 31:6)

577. God (Joshua 1:9)

578. False (Joshua 1:10–15)

579. True (Joshua 10:25)

580. when David instructed Solomon to build the temple (1 Chronicles 22:6–14)

581. a) Assyria (2 Chronicles 32:7)

582. Corinth (1 Corinthians 16:13)

583. c) needed water (Genesis 21:17)

584. d) feared revenge (Genesis 50:19)

585. e) became the leader (Joshua 1:9)

586. f) fear of death (Judges 6:22–23)

587. a) commanded to build the temple (1 Chronicles 22:11, 13)

588. b) afraid of being attacked (Acts 18:9–10)

589. turning water into wine (John 2:1–11)

590. b) Mary (John 2:3)

591. 153 (John 21:11)

592. sleeping in the boat (Mark 4:38)

593. "Peace! Be still!" (Mark 4:39 ESV)

594. True (Mark 6:38)

595. b) Andrew (John 6:8-9)

596. twelve (John 6:13)

597. Jesus walking on the sea, but they supposed it was a spirit and cried out (Mark 6:48–49)

598. raising Lazarus from the dead (John 11:44–53)

599. Joshua, Hezekiah (Joshua 10:12–13; 2 Kings 20:10–11)

600. Enoch, Elijah (Genesis 5:24; 2 Kings 2:1, 11)

601. c) curing a lame man (Acts 3:4–8; 14:8–10)

602. Elisha (2 Kings 4:38, 42–44)

603. Elisha (2 Kings 2:21–22)

604. b) Horeb (Exodus 3:1)

605. He brought him back to life (Luke 7:14–15)

606. He raised Dorcas, also known as Tabitha, from the dead (Acts 9:36–40).

607. c) the sun stood still (Joshua 10:9–14)

608. that their names were written in heaven (Luke 10:19–20)

609. a) bringing forth gnats to cover men and beasts (Exodus 8:18 NASB)

610. a) made the sun stand still and stopped the moon (Joshua 10:13)

611. Gideon (Judges 7:15-16)

612. fellowship (1 John 1:7)

613. Jesus (Matthew 5:14 NLT)

614. so they will praise God (Matthew 5:16)

615. basket, stand (Matthew 5:15 NLT)

616. the seven churches

617. hidden, darkness (1 Corinthians 4:5 NKJV)

618. True. God listens to us any time of the day or night. Sometimes we might say a quick prayer when we need help. Other times, we might utter a short prayer of thanks for a beautiful day or a special blessing. Still on other occasions God may lead us to say a prayer even though we weren't thinking of praying to Him even moments before. No matter how many quick prayers we say during the day, though, it is always good to take time with the Lord each day for a time of unhurried prayer.

619. a) praise Him. God likes for us to glorify and praise Him. This is shown by the many sacrifices He required in the Old Testament.

620. Psalms

621. a) David

623. False. Check out Genesis 24:12, Genesis 25:21, and 1 Samuel 8:6. And there are many more examples.

624. True (Genesis 24:12)

625. d) Rebekah to have a baby (Genesis 25:21)

626. a) be humble. Each and every one of us is lowly in comparison to God. By admitting this to God, we are showing Him we know He is great.

628. True (Jonah 2:1)

629. True (Matthew 26:39). Sometimes God wants us to do something we don't want to do.

630. True. See Mark 1:35 as one example. Jesus got up before the sun rose to spend time alone with God. This may have been the only time He had to be alone with God the Father during an average day.

631. b) alone (Luke 5:16)

632. a) loudly, boasting about his goodness (Luke 18:11)

633. d) all of the above (Matthew 5:43-44)

634. True. When you pray to God, always remember to thank Him for His goodness and mercy as well. There are many examples of thanks given in prayer in the Bible. They are most evident in Psalms since that is a book of praise and prayer.

636. Job (Job 38:4)

637. Adam (Genesis 3:9)

638. Cain (Genesis 4:6)

639. Moses (Exodus 4:2)

640. Solomon (1 Kings 3:5)

641. Satan (Job 1:7)

642. Jonah (Jonah 4:4)

643. Israel (Micah 6:3)

644. Isaiah (Isaiah 6:8)

645. Abraham (Genesis 18:14)

647. a) seven (2 Kings 11:1-4)

648. a) eight (2 Kings 22:1)

649. twelve (Luke 8:42)

650. c) heritage (Psalm 127:3 ESV)

651. a) Hannah (1 Samuel 1:27 NKJV)

652. in the way he should go (Proverbs 22:6)

653. Samuel (1 Samuel 3:10 NKJV)

654. all their births were divinely announced
(Genesis 16:11; 17:19; Judges 13:5; Luke 1:13, 31)

655. a) animals

656. True. The story of Jesus' birth is also found in Luke.

658. b) Joseph (Matthew 1:18)

659. an angel of the Lord (Luke 1:28-33)

660. True (Luke 1:39-40)

661. True (Matthew 1:20)

663. Bethlehem (Luke 2:4-7)

664. b) a census was being taken (Luke 2:1-3). A census is a count of how many people are living in a place at a certain time in history. The United States government takes a census of everyone in the country every ten years. Looking at old census records is one way to find out about your own ancestors.

665. False. King Herod was jealous of the new baby because Jesus was called King of the Jews (Matthew 2:1-3).

666. gold, frankincense, myrrh (Matthew 2:11)

667. False. There was no room for them in the inn (Luke 2:7).

668. c) angels (Luke 2:8-14)

670. False. God warned them in a dream not to go back to King Herod. They returned to their country by another road (Matthew 2:12).

671. False. She had been told what to name Jesus (Luke 2:21).

672. a) Egypt (Matthew 2:13)

673. d) died (Matthew 2:14–15)

675. Nazarene. This is in keeping with the word of the prophets about the Messiah (Matthew 2:23).

676. True (Luke 2:24)

677. c) it was required by Mosaic law (Luke 2:24). The freedom we enjoy as Christians did not come about until after Jesus' ministry and resurrection.

678. Simeon (Luke 2:25). Upon seeing the baby, Simeon told Mary and Joseph that Jesus was the Messiah.

679. b) Jerusalem (Luke 2:22)

680. True. He was proclaimed the Messiah by Simeon and also Anna the prophetess (Luke 2:22-38).

682. True

683. d) Nazareth (Luke 2:39)

684. c) Passover (Luke 2:45)

685. three days (Luke 2:45)

686. a) in the temple, amazing the teachers with His wisdom (Luke 2:46)

687. True. He answered them, "How is it that ye sought me? wist ye not that I must be about my Father's business?" (Luke 2:49 KJV). This means, "Why did you look for me? Didn't you know I was doing my Father's work?"

688. a) John the Baptist. Before John the Baptist was born, he jumped for joy upon hearing of Jesus' impending birth (Luke 1:41). He baptized Jesus (Matthew 3:13–17; Mark 1:9–11; Luke 3:21–22; John 1:31–34). Jesus spoke about John the Baptist after John's death (Matthew 11:12–19; Luke 7:19–35).

690. d) locusts and wild honey (Mark 1:6)

691. True (Matthew 3:11–12)

692. True (Mark 1:8)

693. c) was evil (Luke 3:19)

694. He was put into prison (Luke 3:20).

695. John the Baptist (Matthew 3:13–17; Mark 1:9–11; Luke 3:21–22; John 1:31–34)

696. d) a dove (Luke 3:21–22)

697. False. Instead, Jesus told Satan that people need more than bread. They also need God's Word (Matthew 4:4).

698. c) Jesus was very hungry and wanted to eat because He had not eaten for forty days (Matthew 4:1–3). Satan thought Jesus' hunger would cause Him to give in to this temptation. Satan was mistaken.

699. True (Matthew 4:5–7)

700. a) all the world's kingdoms (Matthew 4:9)

701. angels (Matthew 4:11)

703. Galilee (Luke 4:14)

704. False (Luke 6:35)

705. a) our enemies, without expecting anything in return (Luke 6:35)

706. False (Luke 6:35). Sometimes when you are nice to your enemies, you may feel as though your reward is even more insult and injury. Since this is a fallen world, people are not always nice to you just because you are nice to them. However, sometimes God allows you to receive an earthly reward when a person you are nice to changes his or her mind and becomes your friend. Whether or not this happens, though, those who follow Jesus' teachings will be rewarded in heaven as He promises.

707. c) is kind to everyone, including the evil and unthankful (Luke 6:35)

708. True (Matthew 5:44). Since this teaching goes against the ways of the sinful world, it is probably best to bless your enemies in private. Pray alone to God about them. Talk about it with another Christian you trust.

709. a) tax collector

711. False. Jesus put His teachings into practice. People did not expect the Son of God to eat freely with sinners but to seek out the righteous (Mark 2:15–17).

712. d) go the extra mile for our enemies and show them much love (Luke 6:29)

713. False (Luke 6:37). God is everyone's ultimate judge, and He knows each person's heart. The issue of forgiveness is for Him to decide. God will remember how we respond to other people when it is time for Him to reward us in heaven.

714. b) everyone. Jesus means *all* people, regardless of where they live, and regardless of whether you like them or not.

715. c) love God with all your heart, soul, and mind (Matthew 22:37)

716. b) love one another (John 13:34–35)

717. Judas Iscariot

718. c) thirty pieces of silver (Matthew 26:15). Note: Thirty pieces of silver was worth about 120 denarii, or four months' wages in the first century.

719. a) "Friend, do what you came to do" (Matthew 26:50 ESV). Even in His time of betrayal, Jesus still addressed Judas as "friend." This shows how Jesus followed His own difficult teachings regarding enemies.

721. a) those who didn't love God wouldn't understand His teachings (Matthew 13:11-13)

722. False (Matthew 13:36)

723. the unforgiving servant (Matthew 18:22-35)

724. basket, bed (Mark 4:21 ESV)

725. four (Matthew 13:3-8)

726. birds, the sun, thorns (Matthew 13:4-7)

727. b) Lazarus (Luke 16:19-20)

728. a stone (Luke 11:11 KJV)

729. the kingdom of heaven (Matthew 13:31)

730. Jesus (Luke 15:11-32)

731. False

733. two (Luke 15:11)

734. a) give him his share of his inheritance (Luke 15:12)

735. b) property that is passed on when someone dies

736. True (Luke 15:11–12)

737. c) wasted his money (Luke 15:13)

738. d) tending pigs (Luke 15:15)

739. False. The father ran to the son, hugged him, and kissed him (Luke 15:20).

740. d) a ring, a robe, and shoes (Luke 15:22)

741. True (Luke 15:23–24)

742. False. He begged the older son to join the party (Luke 15:28).

743. d) was angry (Luke 15:28)

744. He was upset because he had not been rewarded with a party, even though he had been faithful and had never strayed from the father (Luke 15:29–30).

745. c) "Everything I have is yours and we are close." (Luke 15:31)

746. True. The father said the younger brother had been lost, but was found. He had been dead, but was alive (Luke 15:32).

747. Luke 10:25-37

749. d) "Who is my neighbor?" (Luke 10:29)

750. a) a lawyer (Luke 10:25)

751. c) had been beaten and robbed (Luke 10:30)

752. False (Luke 10:31-32)

753. Jericho (Luke 10:30)

754. the Samaritan (Luke 10:33)

756. True (Luke 10:35)

757. c) an inn (Luke 10:34)

758. two denarii (Luke 10:35)

760. True. The lawyer said the neighbor was the person who showed mercy (Luke 10:36-37).

761. The Samaritan acted as a neighbor.

762. d) "Go and do likewise" (Luke 10:37 NIV). This means we should be kind to people in need whether or not they belong to our group.

764. a) the Gospels

765. False. He told the man not to tell anyone but to go directly to the priest and offer the sacrifice required under Moses' law (Matthew 8:1–4).

766. d) giving an order for him to be healed. Jesus healed the officer's servant merely by ordering him to get well (Matthew 8:5–13; Luke 7:1–10). This was unusual because Jesus did not even enter the officer's house to see or touch the servant.

768. Jesus healed Peter's mother-in-law (Matthew 8:14–15). Peter is called Simon in Mark 1:30–31 and Luke 4:38–39, which also record this particular healing.

769. b) touching her hand (Matthew 8:14–15; Mark 1:30–31; Luke 4:38–39)

771. True (Luke 4:41)

772. a) herd of pigs (Matthew 8:28–34; Mark 5:1–20; Luke 8:26–39)

773. b) were afraid (Mark 5:15; Luke 8:35)

774. True (Matthew 8:34; Mark 5:17; Luke 8:37)

775. he wanted to go with Jesus (Mark 5:18; Luke 8:38)

776. True (Mark 5:19; Luke 8:39)

777. Yes (Mark 5:20)

778. a) clothing (Matthew 9:20; Mark 5:28; Luke 8:44)

779. d) faith (Matthew 9:22; Mark 5:34; Luke 8:48)

780. True. In fact, preparations were already being made for her funeral (Matthew 9:23).

781. sleeping (Matthew 9:24; Mark 5:39; Luke 8:52)

782. b) two blind men (Matthew 9:27-29)

783. Jesus told them not to tell anyone (Matthew 9:30).

784. No. Word of the healing spread everywhere (Matthew 9:31).

786. The Lord's Prayer appears in both Matthew and Luke. The version from Matthew 6:9-13 is quoted here from the King James Version:

> *Our Father which art in heaven, Hallowed be thy name. Thy kingdom come, Thy will be done in earth, as it is in heaven. Give us this day our daily bread. And forgive us our debts, as we forgive our debtors. And lead us not into temptation, but deliver us from evil: For thine is the kingdom, and the power, and the glory, for ever. Amen.*

787. a) one of them had asked Him to teach them how to pray (Luke 11:1)

788. in heaven

789. He means that we should respect, honor, and revere God's holy name.

791. True

792. True (Matthew 6:5)

793. A hypocrite is a person who acts like someone good in public but does evil things when no one else is watching.

794. False. The Lord's Prayer is a model for us to go by. However, sharing our own concerns with God helps us to become closer to Him. God loves you and He wants to hear about your cares. He also likes for you to thank Him for His goodness.

795. This prayer is named "the Lord's Prayer" because Jesus taught it to us.

796. d) God will forgive us when we forgive others (Matthew 6:14–15)

797. False. Those who pray in the open to get praise already have their reward (Matthew 6:5).

799. poor in spirit (Matthew 5:3 ESV)

800. mourn (Matthew 5:4 ESV)

801. meek (Matthew 5:5 ESV)

802. righteousness (Matthew 5:6 ESV)

803. merciful (Matthew 5:7 ESV)

804. pure in heart (Matthew 5:8 ESV)

805. peacemakers (Matthew 5:9 ESV)

806. persecuted (Matthew 5:10 ESV)

807. evil (Matthew 5:11 ESV)

808. reward (Matthew 5:12 ESV)

810. True

811. True. You can read about them in the Gospels. Some of them are recorded in Luke 4:31-41; 5:12-26; 6:6-11, 17-19.

812. a) tax collectors and outcasts. Some religious leaders in Jesus' day did not understand why the Messiah would spend time with tax collectors and outcasts (Luke 5:30). In Jesus' day, tax collectors often kept much of the tax money for themselves and were thought to be stealing from others.

813. True (Luke 6:1-5)

814. c) a man with a paralyzed hand. Although Jesus knew He was being watched by enemies who were hoping He would break the Jewish law about the Sabbath, Jesus healed the man anyway. Jesus said it was lawful to do good on the Sabbath. Again, this showed how Jesus valued people more than rules (Luke 6:6-10).

815. False. Jesus' enemies were angry that He had broken the Jewish law (Luke 6:11).

816. a) a follower

817. Jesus' disciples are named in Luke 6:13–16. They are:
    Simon, whom He named Peter
    Andrew, Simon's brother
    James
    John
    Philip
    Bartholomew
    Matthew
    Thomas
    James, son of Alphaeus
    Simon, who was called the Patriot (or the Zealot)
    Judas, son of James
    Judas Iscariot, who became the traitor

818. the Sermon on the Mount, also known as the Beatitudes (Luke 6:20–26)

819. False. Jesus said we should love our enemies (Luke 6:27).

820. This means you should treat everyone else the same way you would like them to treat you.

821. False. We should be careful about how we judge other people, because God will judge us by the same standards we use for others (Luke 6:37–42).

822. a) washed His feet with her tears (Luke 7:36-37)

823. d) thought that Jesus shouldn't let a sinful woman touch Him (Luke 7:39)

824. True (Luke 7:47)

825. "Your sins are forgiven." (Luke 7:48 NIV)

826. False. Luke lists several women who followed Jesus, including Mary Magdalene, Joanna, and Susanna, as well as other unnamed women (Luke 8:1-3).

827. False. Jesus said that His family are those who hear and obey God (Luke 8:21). This does not mean we are not to love and honor our families, but that we are to be close to people who love the Lord, whether or not they are family members.

828. a) John the Baptist. John the Baptist was a cousin of Jesus whose ministry was legendary. Some people also thought that Jesus was Elijah or another prophet come back to life (Luke 9:7-9, 18-19).

829. "brought back to life from the dead"

830. True (Luke 9:21-22)

832. d) Moses and Elijah (Luke 9:30-31). This was amazing because both Moses and Elijah had long been dead.

833. Jesus' visitors talked to Him about how He would soon fulfill God's plan for Him (Luke 9:31).

835. b) were afraid and told no one (Luke 9:36)

836. True (Luke 9:46)

837. Jesus said that the person who is the least important on earth is the most important person in heaven (Luke 9:48). This is an important teaching of Jesus because it is the opposite of what the world teaches and it even goes against our own human nature. Rather than looking to be the most important person in the world, it is better for us to put Jesus first.

838. a) told him to stop. They were upset because he was not part of their group (Luke 9:49).

840. False. The Samaritan village did not want Jesus to come through there because He was on His way to Jerusalem. James and John asked Jesus if He wanted them to command fire to come from heaven to destroy the village (Luke 9:54).

841. c) not to be unforgiving toward the citizens of the town (Luke 9:55)

842. False. Jesus and the disciples went another way (Luke 9:56).

844. d) nothing (Luke 10:4)

845. The workers would be taken care of by the people in each town. They were told to go to a house and greet the people living there with peace. Those people were to give them food and shelter during their stay in the town.

846. a) lambs among wolves (Luke 10:3)

847. True (Luke 10:17)

849. Mark 16:1 names Mary Magdalene, Mary the mother of James, and Salome. There were other unnamed women. Luke 24:10 names Joanna.

850. a) an angel of the Lord (Matthew 28:2)

851. c) "Fear not, for Jesus has risen" (Matthew 28:5–6). Note: An earthquake had already happened when the angel rolled away the stone (Matthew 28:2).

852. False (Luke 24:11)

853. Peter and John

854. True (John 20:11–18)

855. c) "Peace be unto you." (John 20:19 KJV)

856. c) wanted to reassure them. They were hiding because they feared they would be killed for following Jesus (John 20:19).

857. False. People can be persecuted for many reasons, but it is those who are tormented for being Christians who will inherit the kingdom of heaven (Matthew 5:10).

858. the prophets (Matthew 5:12)

859. the book of Acts

860. False (Acts 6:8)

862. a) blasphemy (Acts 6:11)

863. False. Stephen's enemies could not defeat his wisdom in open debate, so they convinced some men to lie about Stephen (Acts 6:9–11).

864. c) like an angel (Acts 6:15)

865. d) giving a speech in defense of Christianity (Acts 7:1–53)

866. False (Acts 7:51–53). Stephen was saying that Israel was not faithful to the Lord, even though they were His chosen people.

867. c) the glory of God and Jesus at God's right hand in heaven (Acts 7:56)

868. because he told everyone what he saw (Acts 7:56)

869. a) angry (Acts 7:57–58)

870. True (Acts 7:60)

871. the apostle Paul

872. b) members of the church at Corinth. Paul's letters to them gave advice on how they should live as Christians.

874. False. Without love, any speech is just a lot of noise (1 Corinthians 13:1).

875. False. You must have love (1 Corinthians 13:2–3).

876. d) proud (1 Corinthians 13:4). This means you will let the person you love be first, or the most important.

877. This means if you love someone, it will take a lot to make you mad at that person.

878. False (1 Corinthians 13:8–9)

879. love (1 Corinthians 13:13)

880. c) a set of attitudes you'll have if you love God

881. Galatians 5:22–23

882. the apostle Paul

883. a) members of a group of churches in Galatia

885. 1 Corinthians 13

886. b) happiness in the Lord

888. c) you can forgive other people when they sin against you

890. True (Galatians 5:22)

891. False. No matter what, a person of faith always believes in God (Hebrews 11:1).

892. False (Galatians 5:18). He wanted to show that Christian conduct is more important than following the law.

893. d) don't think about their bodies as much as they think about living for Christ (Galatians 5:24–25)

894. a) we obey Christ

895. False. Christians should not seek others' possessions (Galatians 5:26).

896. There are many good reasons to obey Christ. In Galatians, Paul is showing us how we will act if we are obedient. Loving others is a good way to be an ambassador for Christ.

897. love, joy, peace, patience, kindness, goodness, faithfulness, gentleness, and self-control (Galatians 5:22–23)

898. False (Acts 8:1). Paul persecuted early Christians before becoming a Christian himself.

899. c) members of the church at Ephesus

901. Paul himself tells us he wrote the letter in the first verse (Ephesians 1:1).

902. False (Ephesians 3:8)

903. c) Gentiles and Jews are equal. Christ died for all who love Him, not just for one certain group of people (Ephesians 3:6).

904. True (Ephesians 4:6)

905. d) Christians

906. be honest with each other, but in a kind way, never trying to hurt each other's feelings

908. c) righteousness

909. b) salvation

910. d) gospel of peace

911. f) truth

912. a) Word of God

913. e) faith

914. Aquila and Priscilla (Acts 18:24–26)

915. Paul (Acts 22:3)

916. Eli (1 Samuel 3:1)

917. a) his grandma and his mom (2 Timothy 1:5)

918. the younger women

919. the Christ (Matthew 23:8)

920. Nicodemus (John 3:2 NKJV)

921. Antioch (Acts 11:26)

922. Aquila and Priscilla (Acts 18:1–2)

923. c) Thyatira (Acts 16:14)

924. elders (Acts 14:23)

925. True (Acts 13:1)

926. Antioch (Acts 13:1–3)

927. Ephesus, Smyrna, Pergamum, Thyatira, Sardis, Philadelphia, Laodicea (Revelation 2–3)

928. Ephesus (Revelation 2:1, 4)

929. Laodicea (Revelation 3:14, 16)

930. Thyatira (Revelation 2:18, 20)

931. Pergamum (Revelation 2:12–13)

932. Sardis (Revelation 3:1)

934. d) John Mark (Romans 1:1; Matthew 10:2–4; Acts 1:26)

935. They were given miraculous powers (Matthew 10:1).

936. The apostles will judge the tribes (Matthew 19:28).

937. Peter (Acts 2:1, 14)

938. d) all of the above (Acts 10:1-2)

939. False. Only eleven; Judas wasn't an apostle (Acts 1:25)

940. Some would be killed and persecuted (Luke 11:49).

941. d) a & b (Acts 2:42)

942. d) all the material things they wanted to share (Acts 4:34-35)

943. False (Acts 8:1)

944. Barnabas (Acts 9:27)

945. True (Acts 14:14)

946. He was called (1 Corinthians 1:1).

947. least (1 Corinthians 15:9)

948. True (Hebrews 3:1)

949. True (Galatians 2:11-14)

950. a) Peter

951. True

952. b) is named first in every list of the apostles in the Bible. These lists are found in Matthew 10:2-4, Mark 3:13-19, Luke 6:12-16, and Acts 1:13-14.

953. b) persecuted Christians (1 Peter 1:1)

954. d) eternal life. The Christian looks forward to living with God in heaven rather than having lots of things here.

955. True (1 Peter 1:14). Jesus' teachings go against the world's system of greed and materialism. Instead of encouraging us to get more stuff, He tells us God will provide for our needs. When we trust God, there is no need to be greedy or to wish we had more than someone else.

956. *Redeemed* means "saved." Those who accept Jesus' gift of salvation are saved and forgiven for their sins.

957. a) Jesus (1 Peter 1:7-9). Jesus redeemed us when He was crucified on the cross.

958. a) newborn babies (1 Peter 2:2). This means we should desire the pure milk of the Word of God, which is the Bible.

959. d) make Christians grow (1 Peter 2:2). The more we read the Bible, the more we learn about Jesus and the Christian faith.

960. c) living stones (1 Peter 2:5)

961. True (1 Peter 2:5)

962. True

963. stone (1 Peter 2:6–7). This means Jesus is the foundation of our faith.

964. This means people who don't want to obey Jesus will trip over His Word and find it insulting and offensive.

965. True. We are ambassadors for Christ. Our conduct should cause unbelievers to praise the Lord (1 Peter 2:11–12).

966. A sojourner is a guest. We are guests in this world, because our true home is in heaven with the Lord. We can enjoy God's awesome creation while we live here.

967. b) obey the laws of their nations (1 Peter 2:13). If we obey the law, no one can say we think we are above the law. Christians are obligated to be good citizens.

968. False (1 Peter 2:18). We are to forgive others.

969. a) remember how Jesus trusted God. Jesus did not insult people who insulted Him; He trusted God (1 Peter 2:23–24).

970. c) lost sheep (1 Peter 2:25). This means they were sinners who had gotten away from God.

971. Psalm 23

972. False. Beauty from within is precious to God (1 Peter 3:3-4).

973. True (1 Peter 3:14). Peter wrote this to encourage Christians who were suffering just for being Christians. Some important people in the government did not like Christians, and they tried to make their lives difficult. Sometimes people were even killed for being Christians.

974. b) meekness (1 Peter 3:15-16)

976. True (1 Peter 4:12-16)

977. b) elders (1 Peter 5:5)

978. the devil (1 Peter 5:8)

980. a) Christians in Asia Minor (2 Peter 1:1)

981. True (2 Peter 1:3-4)

982. faith, virtue, knowledge, self-control, perseverance, godliness, brotherly kindness, and love (2 Peter 1:5-7). Can you think of someone who is like this? Think about how Christians can display these characteristics in real life.

984. True (2 Peter 1:16–18)

985. False. False prophets will be punished (2 Peter 2:12–13).

986. d) all of the above (2 Peter 2:1–3)

987. b) as a thief in the night (2 Peter 3:10). This means it will be unexpected. Do not listen to anyone who claims to know the exact day the Lord will return. Not even Jesus knew the date while He lived on earth (Matthew 24:36).

988. True. We must stay faithful to God's Word (2 Peter 3:17).

989. It is important to study all sixty-six books of the Bible. Peter's letters are important because they give us instructions on how to live as Christians.

990. a) ourselves (1 John 1:8)

991. death

992. crimson, scarlet (Isaiah 1:18)

993. d) a & b (Isaiah 1:18)

994. b) as far as east is from west

995. when we confess our sins (1 John 1:9)

996. salvation (Psalm 27:1 ESV)

997. d) with nothing; His gift of salvation is free

998. to believe in Him (John 3:16)

999. mouth, heart (Romans 10:9 ESV)

ABOUT THE EDITORS

Jodi and Lilly Simmons are sisters who live in Ohio with their parents and two funny dogs named Jasper and Daisy, who are hilarious when they play tug-of-war. Jodi is ten years old and likes the beach, art, dancing, swimming, and reading. Lilly is eight years old and likes music, dolls, dancing, and making new friends. Jodi and Lilly also helped their mom write a devotional called *How God Grows a Girl of Grace*.

Continue the Fun with...

999 SUPER SILLY, AWESOMELY HILARIOUS, FUNNY BONE-TICKLING JOKES FOR KIDS

Kids love to laugh—and here's a fantastic collection of more than 999 jokes and funny stories especially for 6- to 12-year-olds! Compiled and edited *by kids for kids,* you can be sure these are jokes that young readers will find a ton of laughs to enjoy and share—with anyone who will listen! *999 Super Silly, Awesomely Hilarious, Funny Bone-Tickling Jokes for Kids* promises hours of good, wholesome entertainment for the whole family!

Paperback / 978-1-68322-561-4 / $4.99